LIVING WITH BIPOLAR DISORDER

Strategies for Balance and Resilience

LIVING WITH
BIPOLAR DISORDER

Strategies for Balance and Resilience

Lynn Hodges

 FINDHORN PRESS

© Lynn Hodges 2012

The right of Lynn Hodges to be identified as the author
of this work has been asserted by her in accordance
with the Copyright, Designs and Patents Act 1998.

Published in 2012 by Findhorn Press, Scotland

ISBN 978-1-84409-586-5

A CIP record for this title is available from the British Library.

Edited by Nicky Leach
Cover design by Richard Crookes
Illustrations by Lynn Hodges
Interior design by Damian Keenan
Printed and bound in the USA

1 2 3 4 5 6 7 8 9 17 16 15 14 13 12

Published by
Findhorn Press
117-121 High Street,
Forres IV36 1AB,
Scotland, UK

t +44 (0)1309 690582
f +44 (0)131 777 2711
e info@findhornpress.com
www.findhornpress.com

Acknowledgements

I first want to say a big thank you to my three children—Megan, Brooke, and Zac—who manage my illness brilliantly.

Thanks go to Millie Thompson, a young lady who freely gave her time to help me research information needed for this book.

My thanks also go to my sister, Kay Taylor. She has been there to offer ideas, proofread text, and generally be a sounding board.

My sister, Jill Gare, has kept me going when I have lost confidence. She has been instrumental in making sure I never gave up.

Thanks to Elaine Everest of *www.thewriteplace.org.uk,* for giving me the knowledge of how to find a publisher and interest them in my work.

I want to say a very big thank you to all the patients who were happy to share their stories for this book.

My care coordinator Kate Rawlings deserves my thanks for listening to me and giving me advice and knowledge on understanding things from the health professional's perspective.

I also want to say thank you to Findhorn Press for believing in me, especially to Sabine Weeke, who held my hand every step of the way.

My thanks go to Nicky Leach, my editor: without her I would not have been able to produce such a cohesive message.

Lastly, I'd like to thank my friends Barbara Harrison, Sally Smith, Linda Bennett, and Karen Rayment, who are instrumental in keeping me well. Their humour and good grace have played a large part in my life. After all, where are we without good friends?

Contents

Contents

Contents

The Evacuee

Introduction

Did you know that one in four people in the United Kingdom will experience a mental health problem in their lifetime, and on average 1.3 percent of the population of the UK will at some point develop manic depression, now known as bipolar disorder?

Most people first become unwell with bipolar disorder when they are in their mid-teens and twenties. However, as bipolar is so difficult to diagnose, it is common for many people to go a decade or more without receiving a formal medical diagnosis. Some ten percent of all teenagers with recurring depression will go on to develop bipolar disorder during their lives.

The illness can affect anyone—from the young to the very old, male or female. It is important to know about and understand the condition, so you feel better equipped to deal with the illness. Information is power in dealing with this disease.

This is a self-help book for people who are newly diagnosed with bipolar disorder, as well as for those individuals who have had the illness for some time. The information in the book is also designed to help the family and friends of people with bipolar gain a better understanding of the condition. I hope, too, that my personal story of dealing with bipolar will be of interest to health professionals who wish to help clients managing the disease.

The book offers stories and insights into my own journey with bipolar, as well as those of others with the disorder. Throughout you will find tips and guidance on how to live with this illness and keep in recovery as long as possible.

Living with bipolar disorder is not all bad. I have lived a very successful life in spite of having bipolar. I worked in an advertising agency during my younger years, and then ran my own successful presentation company, Up Front, for 20 years. I now run Creative Coaching Consultancy, a company specializing in working with doctors, psychiatrists, social workers, and all those involved in mental health services to help them understand what it is like to live with bipolar disorder.

Creativity is an integral part of bipolar and, during the course of the book, I explain why I would not wish to be free of this illness, even if you offered me a million pounds for it to go away.

CHAPTER ONE

What is Bipolar Disorder?

Bipolar disorder was once known as manic depression. There are good reasons for changing the name. The word "manic" scared many people and labelled the mentally ill as "mad."

The National Institute of Mental Health (NIMH) in the United States describes bipolar disorder as follows:

> Bipolar Disorder, also known as Manic Depressive Illness, is a brain disorder that causes unusual shifts in mood, energy, activity levels, and the ability to carry out day-to-day tasks. Symptoms of Bipolar Disorder are severe. They are different from the normal ups and downs that everyone goes through from time to time. Bipolar Disorder symptoms can result in damaged relationships, poor job or school performance and even suicide. **Bipolar Disorder *can* be treated, and people with this illness do lead full and productive lives**.

The Diagnostic & Statistical Manual of Mental Disorders (DSM-IV-TR), used by psychiatrists and general practitioners (GPs) in the US and UK, offers the following description of the mania, hypomania, and depression associated with bipolar disorder:

Mania

- Extreme elevated mood or euphoria
- Grandiosity
- High energy

- Irritability
- Rapid speech
- Racing thoughts
- Decreased sleep
- Impulsiveness
- Risky sexual behaviours
- Excessive spending

Hypomania

Specifically, hypomania is distinguished from mania by the absence of psychotic symptoms and grandiosity, and by its lesser degree of impact on functioning.

Hypomania is a feature of Bipolar II Disorder and Cyclothymia, but can also occur in Schizoaffective Disorder. Hypomania is also a feature of Bipolar I Disorder as it arises in sequential procession as the mood disorder fluctuates between normal mood and mania.

Some individuals with Bipolar I Disorder have hypomanic as well as manic episodes. Hypomania can also occur when moods progress downwards from a manic mood state to a normal mood.

Hypomania is sometimes credited with increasing creativity and productive energy. A significant number of people with creative talents have reportedly experienced hypomania or other symptoms of Bipolar Disorder and attribute their success to it.

Classic symptoms of hypomania include:

- Mild euphoria
- A flood of ideas
- Endless energy
- Desire and drive for success

Depression

The mania is accompanied with one or more depressive episodes. The depressive episodes seen in Bipolar, in contrast to those seen typically in a major depression, tend to come on fairly acutely, over perhaps a few weeks, and often occur without any significant precipitating factors.

They tend to be characterized by psychomotor retardation hyperphagia, and hypersomnolence and are not uncommonly accompanied by delusions or hallucinations.

On average, untreated these Bipolar depressions tend to last about six months.

DSM-IV-TR goes on to explain that there are two types of Bipolar Disorders: Bipolar I and Bipolar II:

> People with Bipolar I Disorder suffer from alterations of full manic episodes and major depressive episodes.
> On the contrary people with Bipolar II Disorder experience a milder form of a manic episode, known as a hypomanic episode, as well as experiencing major depressive episodes.
>
> Although Bipolar II is thought to be less severe than Bipolar I in regards to symptom intensity, it is actually more severe and distressing with respect to episode frequency and overall course.
>
> Cyclothymia is a mood and mental disorder in the Bipolar spectrum that causes both hypomania and depressive episodes. It is defined medically within the Bipolar spectrum and consists of recurrent disturbances between sudden hypomania and dysthymic episodes or mixed episodes.
>
> The lifetime prevalence of cyclothymic disorder is 0.4-1%. The rate appears equal between men and women, though more women often seek treatment. People with Cyclothymia are more often fully functioning.

As you can see from the above medical definitions, there is more to this illness than slipping from mania and hypomania to depression; instead, you travel along the road and reach different destinations on your way. For example, when you travel towards mania, you reach a stage called hypomania. This is a great place to be on the spectrum of the disorder, as the ability to work and communicate increases by more than 75 percent in most people. I know this is true for me. The key is, how does one stay in this state?

Bipolar is often seen as a life sentence: once diagnosed you will never be free of the condition. Bipolar has a lot in common with diabetes, in that you have to manage the condition. But if you can learn to be successful at self-management, there is no reason why you cannot live a very fulfilling life.

Bipolar disorder can be worsened by intense emotional stress. If I become stressed, the chances of me having a bipolar episode increase. Creative people who are demonstrative emotionally are often classified as "highly strung," but the truth is that many talented creative individuals live with bipolar.

The question I often ask myself is: Does the condition and high creativity go hand in hand? I personally think the answer is yes. Over the years I have found myself in very creative positions—professional actress, entrepreneur, professional artist, and writer. I do not think I could do these jobs without the help of bipolar. Over the chapters that follow, we will explore these aspects of the illness.

I have worked very hard to manage my mental attitude about the illness. I cope by treating bipolar disorder as my friend, not my foe. It is never going to leave me—and yes, it plays me up like a naughty child. I have to be firm and learn to believe that I am the boss and together we will get through each and every episode.

Although bipolar disorder is a very serious mental illness and not to be laughed at, humour is, in fact, one of the best short-term cures.

As you read this book, I hope you will find yourself laughing on many occasions.

Accepting the Diagnosis

Accepting the diagnosis has to be the hardest part of the journey. I was diagnosed with Bipolar I in May 2004, after a manic episode that led me into The Little Brook Hospital, Dartford, Kent, in England.

I do believe that I had been misdiagnosed earlier in my life. I was born in 1961, and I was 30 years old when I had my first major depression, which put me into a psychiatric ward for six weeks. The diagnosis then was depression with psychosis.

I had always been known as the one who was "off the wall," always doing half-crazy things, like singing half-naked in a park at midnight, a nonconformist.

Once, whilst waiting in a queue in Nat West Bank with the rest of the customers, I decided to sit on the floor. I caused such a stir. People kept coming up to me asking if I was alright. I explained I just wanted to sit rather than stand, as I was fed up with waiting. A Nat West customer service staff member eventually came to the rescue. She could not deal with the situation, so she decided to leap-frog me to the front of the queue.

Looking back, I wonder now if this was normal behaviour on my part, or was I showing the signs of bipolar many years ago?

I believe now that I have had the illness since I was 21 years old. At the time, I was working for a very exciting, creative advertising agency called Collett Dickenson & Pearce. On the occasion of my 21st, my work colleagues decided to throw a party for me to celebrate this special milestone. My parents had been invited to the work party, and since my mother and father had been divorced for some time, my mother decided to come on her own.

It turned out to be a very bad decision.

I consumed a fair amount of alcohol and started to dance like mad. I then decided to go to the DJ and ask him to stop the music, as I wanted to give a speech. This did not seem a bad thing to do at the time, except what came from my lips will always stay with me. I decided to announce my mother as part of my anatomy, "A 'c**t!!'" The part of the body that God gave us to have babies! That is what she was to me.

As you can imagine, the room went completely silent. No one knew what to do. I was saved by my boss, who took to the floor to announce that all 21-year-olds had the right to embarrass their parents, and this was certainly what had happened on this occasion. My mother has never once mentioned that night since. I must have hurt her very much, and if I could change that moment I would. Having bipolar disorder really *does* mean having to say sorry. It was definitely an occasion when I should have apologized.

Another strange incident happened when I was 27 years old. I was on holiday in Greece with my very dear friend Barbara, and we had taken out a small boat so we could sunbathe. Whilst on the boat, we came across a ship moored with half the British navy on board—well, we thought they were British. Within minutes, I had taken all my clothes off and started dancing and prancing around. I always liked to have fun, but this behaviour was extreme.

My friend knew me and my antics well and was able to calm me down and get us out of muddy waters. The men on the boat were beside themselves, shouting for us to come over so they could see how much farther we were willing to go. Thank goodness I was not on my own or the story could have been so different.

It would have been much better if someone in the health profession had detected my odd behaviour way back then, as people would have been more forgiving. Unfortunately, I put it down to my excessive personality and did not even think about visiting a doctor to see whether there was more to this.

Although I eventually received the diagnosis of bipolar disorder in 2004, it had taken two decades to get to the bottom of my problem. This is very common, and it is something we can only hope improves with more knowledge of the illness.

Even though I now had an official diagnosis, I still did not want to believe it. Nor did I understand what it meant to have bipolar disorder. I was convinced I was just emotionally unstable and once my mind calmed down all would be okay.

I had good reason for feeling emotional turmoil—I had just split from my children's father after 13 years together and felt cut up about leaving him.

We were living in Spain together, after taking a sabbatical in the hopes of rebuilding our relationship. Unfortunately, living in Spain exposed all my partner's worst characteristics. He drank heavily and found it very hard to say no, whilst I, on the other hand, enjoyed a drink but did not like it to be the focal point of our lives.

Our children were still young—Megan was ten years old, Brooke seven, and Zac four. I found myself travelling back and forth from Spain to London and France to run my business, and every time I returned home, I was unhappy with what I found.

I stayed in Spain for nearly a year hoping things would change, spending thousands of pounds trying to keep the relationship going, watching my children suffer and my business unable to take the pressure of me not being present all the time.

During a visit by my sister Jill and her family, she became concerned about my health—so much so that, returning to Kent two weeks later, Jill asked my other sister, Kay, to come to see me and check out the situation.

When Kay and her family arrived, Kay quickly realized I was unwell. By this stage, I was on antidepressants and not able to operate very well. After long conversations into the night with Kay, I decided to leave my partner and take the children back to England.

I have to be honest—I did not sit down with my partner to explain why I was leaving. He was not in a good place, his drinking was escalating, and he was becoming more agitated. I was anxious not to upset him. I never have felt good about the way in which I left him, but I know the decision was the right one.

After returning to Kent with my children and Kay, I had nowhere to live. My home was being rented out, and it was not possible to get the tenants to vacate it for at least three months. I also did not want to return to that house, which was the family home. I knew in my heart I had to start again. My sisters rose to the occasion brilliantly and allowed my children and me to come and stay with them until I had sorted myself out.

I had been back home just two months when I had my first manic episode. I had been expressing bizarre behaviour for a few weeks and was starting to get out of control. I believed it was stress, but Kay and Jill decided I needed to see a doctor.

Things came to a head one Friday night. I thought by agreeing to visit the doctor I would have my antidepressant medication increased and things would return to normal. Instead, I was marched off to a psychiatric ward.

A few weeks after I had been hospitalized, I was given my diagnosis: Bipolar I. I laughed at this. They were wrong. They were all so very wrong. I was suffering from a broken heart. Why could no one understand this? I believed that the stress of living with my partner and his drinking habits over the previous year, deciding to leave him and take the children, packing up our life's belongings into a few bags, and then having no roof over our heads was the real problem.

In hospital, I was forced to take my medication like clockwork, but I knew that when I left hospital, I would be putting the tablets in the bin. It took me two more episodes of mania to realize the doctors were right: I do have bipolar disorder.

After leaving the hospital, I was cared for by a team of people known as the crisis team whose main role is to keep you out of hospital. They visit and care for you at home. It was the crisis team who convinced me that I did have bipolar, not a broken heart, and that I would have to learn to live with this illness and accept that the diagnosis was correct.

I knew then that I had to learn more about the illness and that I needed to be directed to people who could help me. This does not come easy and everyone needs help with it. Information is, of course, available on the Internet, but unless you know what you are looking for it can be overwhelming. A lot of the material is very depressing—it speaks about the black side of the illness and forgets to mention its positive attributes. My own experience of researching information on the Internet was that I felt very frightened of what the future held.

As I mentioned, the hardest thing for me was accepting that I had a mental illness—if I had been diagnosed with a physical illness, I would have been able to cope better. The fact is, the brain is very complex and each individual with this condition will display many different aspects of the illness. No two cases are the same.

The other aspect of bipolar disorder is that the condition can change and develop over time. Bipolar is like the weather: you can often predict a storm is coming, but no one knows if it will or not. I have more manic episodes than depressions, but that does not mean it will stay like this. All you can do is hope and pray and do your best to control as much of the illness as possible. This is part of what you have to live with each day. The positive side of this is that no two days are the same. It is rare to find yourself bored, as the moods sweep you in different directions.

Knowing that it is possible to live with this illness is helpful, and so is finding out that I am not alone. But the negative information about bipolar made me feel immobilized with worry, and it is this worry that has led me to write this book. I want to be able to allay some of the fears of others with this diagnosis so that they feel better and less alone.

Learning You Are Not Alone

One of the things I found difficult to accept when reading about other people's experiences was the extreme negativity about the illness they experienced. But it's important to remember that after every down there is an up and this condition can help your creativity. In my mind, there is no doubt that bipolar disease and creativity are linked, and whenever you feel isolated, which you often can, it is good to be reminded of this.

The real reason for feeling alone is that it is hard for friends and loved ones to understand your bizarre behaviour. When you are depressed, friends look at your life and do not understand why you feel so low—to them you have everything. The reality, of course, is that an important brain chemical, or neurotransmitter—serotonin—is not getting to the brain. So, like a diabetic without insulin, you are unable to operate effectively.

As a reminder that you are not alone, here is a list of just a few well-known public figures who live with bipolar:

Russell Brand	*Actor*
Frank Bruno	*Boxer*
Richard Dreyfuss	*Actor*
Carrie Fisher	*Actress*
Stephen Fry	*Actor*
Paul Gascoigne	*Footballer*
Catherine Zeta Jones	*Actress*
Graham Greene	*Novelist*
Ernest Hemingway	*Author*
Vivien Leigh	*Actress*

Spike Milligan	*Comedian*
Ozzy Osborne	*Singer*
Edgar Allan Poe	*Poet*
Ruby Wax	*Comedian*

Your behaviour can be so irrational that you worry about rebuilding good relationships with colleagues, friends, and families. Real friends are always there for you, but you may be surprised to find that there are some people who, unfortunately, just can't cope with your diagnosis.

It is not surprising, considering the behaviour that can accompany this disease. I only remember a few of the crazy things I did in the lead-up to my manic episode in 2004 whilst I was living with Kay. They could test anyone's patience.

For example, I had a compulsion to throw away as many of my sister's things as I could—from TV remotes, candles, and clothes to toilet brushes. I would see them and say to myself that she would be better off without all this clutter, then they would end up in a black refuse sack that I would put outside her door!

I also went on a car rampage. One night, I took my children and my sister's son Sam out for dinner. On the way home, I decided that I no longer wanted to be me, so I threw my passport, cheque books, handbag, and Kay's house keys out of the car window as we drove along the A20 at 80 mph.

My nephew Sam, who at the time was about 12 years old and is a very bright boy, asked me why I was throwing my keys away. He was distressed, as they were his house keys and he knew his mum would be very angry. I calmly explained that I had no use for them any longer. He looked at me and his eyes started to well up with tears. He knew something was very wrong.

My nephew, of course, told his mum about the episode, but when I spoke to Kay I managed to convince her that I was depressed and not thinking straight. Kay had also found the items in the black refuse sacks and asked me how they had got there. I apologized and promised it would not happen again.

After this, my sister started watching me like a hawk. I decided I would leave the house early in the morning and come back later at night, hoping this might control my behaviour. Unfortunately, it had the opposite effect.

At the time, my children were attending school in London, so I had to get up early every morning for the long drive to the school and my office. One day, when I was alone at work, I decided I wanted to feel good about myself—in fact, I wanted to feel like a diamond. With that thought firmly in my head I took myself off to a jeweller's. Whilst I was there, I selected a diamond ring that cost £1,200, diamond earrings costing £800, a diamond watch costing £950, and three silver crosses for my children that cost £240. I also picked up eight St Christopher's pendants representing the patron saint of travel.

Why? Well, I had decided I was going to take my children around the world in a motor home and St Christopher would keep them safe.

I had never bought myself diamonds before—this behaviour was definitely not normal. And since the St Christopher's medallions were bought for safety on our travels, to make this a reality I would post a St Christopher in mailboxes all around London when I drove the children to school each morning.

The thought processes behind my actions were becoming more disturbed. I would go into my office and pack up books, remotes, videos, and files and throw them all into black refuse sacks. I cleared the contents in the desks of three out of the five employees working for me and placed them in black refuse sacks. After I had done that, I covered everything in salt, vinegar, ketchup, and pepper—I saw the condiments as essence that God would like and felt that they needed to cover everything in the sacks.

During the next couple of days, I decided to take the children to my holiday caravan on a caravan site in Monkton, near Canterbury, to see if I could relax. I knew at this point that something was seriously wrong, and I hoped that by going to my caravan for a weekend it might help my mind settle.

The weekend started off normally. We had a meal at the local restaurant and turned in for an early night. But I was awakened in the middle of the night by the thought that I needed to purchase a motor home for our travels. I knew we were going to travel; a motor home would be our way of doing it.

Next morning we went on a family walk, and to my surprise a motor home was parked in a driveway for sale. Naturally, I saw this as a sign from God. My children were very excited at the thought of travelling the world and were unaware of my state of mind. Within 30 minutes, I was the owner of a brand new life. It had cost me £13,500 for a 15-year-old motor home.

But I was not even confident enough in my driving skills to drive it out of the driveway. How was I going to drive it around the world? Clearly, this was a question I should have asked myself before making the purchase! I had to get my brother-in-law to drive down to Monkton with his friend and drive the motor home back to my sister's house. You can only imagine her surprise when this 20-foot-long monstrosity arrived in her driveway. If you think she was surprised, imagine her neighbour's response!

To complete the spending spree that weekend, I purchased four extremely expensive laptops, at £1,000 each, for myself and my children. After all, I needed to be able to teach them on our round-the-world trip.

When I returned to Kay's house, the children were excited about the motor home and told their auntie all about it and their forthcoming trip. My sister, understandably, was beside herself and became very upset and angry. She did not know what was happening to me or what to do.

That night I found myself wrapped around my sister's toilet seat, crying. I knew I needed help, but I did not know what was wrong. In the next instant, I had taken the new, beautiful diamonds and started to flush them down her toilet. They all disappeared, except for the beautiful watch, which I fished back out. The diamonds were my secret; no one else was to know.

For the moment, Kay remained completely unaware of the jewellery purchase. But she had heard me crying and came into the toilet to comfort me. It was at that point that I told her that I had flushed the diamonds down her toilet. She was completely aghast. Whatever had I done that for? She just couldn't understand. Being the practical woman she is, the thought of flushing diamonds down the toilet left her completely dizzy!

Kay called a plumber to see if he could retrieve the diamonds. (Imagine that phone call. *Could you please come to the house? I have flushed all my diamonds down the toilet!!*) The plumber came and tried everything, from the toilet to the outside drains, but nothing could be found.

This manic period had now lasted about three weeks, and I was feeling very alone and frightened of what I might do next.

Kay felt enough was enough. She did not know what was happening to me and knew that she needed expert help to figure it out. The following day, she marched me straight down to her local surgery, where the doctor suspected bipolar disorder and that was when I was hospitalized for six weeks.

Feeling alone and out of control are definitely aspects of this illness, and any mess you cause is left to you to sort out. I had spent £25,000 of company money, and somehow I had to repay the debt. Thank heavens it was my company.

Looking on the bright side, I got to experience wearing a diamond ring and diamond jewellery for a few hours, and still to this day I have the lovely watch—the only thing that didn't sink!

Masked

CHAPTER TWO

Depression: The Black Cloud

My most recent depression has lasted five months, and it is amazing how many people tell you to snap out of it. Making comments like that is just not helpful. Depression is a clinical illness and very much part of bipolar disorder.

I have mentioned hypomania as a happy place to be: it may be scary to the people around me, but in my head everything is real and fine. At the other end of the spectrum is depression, which is just awful.

How do you know when you are depressed? First, it is not something you can just snap out of—it's a feeling that just overwhelms you. Here are the signs I recognize as depression:

- Fatigue – Unable to function, keep house clean, and so on;
- Disrupted sleeping patterns – Sleeping all day, or no sleep at all;
- Poor personal hygiene – Not wanting to shower or bathe;
- Extreme eating habits – Either eating to excess or not eating at all;
- Withdrawing – Withdrawing from people and places;
- Having to stay in a place of comfort;
- Anxiety related to any change.

When I am depressed I feel like my whole life is over. I am unable to imagine any future possibilities for my life. I am unable to participate in the smallest activity, from cooking the children dinner, washing, and ironing to reading, painting, or going to work.

As you can imagine, having a depression for five months and not being able to work leaves you in a very weak financial position. I have been very lucky working for Kent County Council in southeast England. They understand that I suffer from bipolar disorder, so I work when I am well and retreat into the background when I am not able to function.

One of the most difficult aspects of depression is that you generally don't wish to see anyone, yet, paradoxically, you need people to help you lift the depression. During this time, it is essential to try to engage with family and friends and to see your social worker or other mental health professional, as they can monitor the severity of the depression and decide on a course of action for you.

When my social worker saw me recently, she was shocked to see how quickly I had slid into a depression. I was facing some real life challenges at the time. They would have made the best of people depressed, but for someone with bipolar disorder, it was particularly overwhelming.

My financial pressures were enormous. I had personal debts caused by bipolar, and in addition, my business had started to decline. As a result, I was selling my London house, which had been our family home prior to living in Spain. I did not want to sell it. That house was to have been my pension, and selling it made me feel financially very vulnerable. But I was in debt with my mortgage company—not only on the house we were living in in Kent but also on my London property.

I was down on my luck, and the stress this caused was triggering depression. My mental health team needed to decide whether my depression was a clinical depression or whether it was brought on by life events.

When I went to see my psychiatrist she asked me lots of questions, and then decided that, because of my financial pressures, initially she would not put me on an antidepressant. She believed that when my house sold and the financial pressure was relieved, I would naturally feel in a much better place. Among her concerns was the possibility that if she adjusted my mood pharmaceutically with antidepressants, there was a chance that I would "spin up high" (go into mania) several weeks later. Since I have a very good relationship with my psychiatrist, I accepted her advice and made an appointment to see her again in two weeks' time.

Unfortunately, over the course of the following two weeks my depression worsened. My eating habits spiralled out of control, and soon I was living on fast food, which did nothing to improve my mood. I slept for 15 hours a day and still felt tired. My anxiety over small things, such as driving the car, got out of hand. I was constantly in a state of panic.

My social worker came round to visit me on a weekly basis and was the one to set off the alarm bells about my downward spiral. She called my psychiatrist and requested that I move up my appointment. When I went in to see my psychiatrist, she was concerned about my condition and changed her mind about antidepressants. She put me on a low-dosage medication that she increased gradually over the next month.

Taking antidepressant medication when you are bipolar is a worry, as it can so easily switch into mania, but being depressed is far worse. I much prefer experiencing hypomania and mania to depression, although people around me may not agree on that point. You don't know how long it is going to last, so friends and family have to be understanding, as do work colleagues.

People often ask me whether it is possible to go to work when you are depressed. My answer is yes, although it depends on the work. As many people realize, work can often be the best cure because it offers a structure to the day that allows you to focus, get out of bed, and push yourself. If you set yourself small goals, work can be attainable.

In fact, when I was asked to write this book I was in a full-blown depression. My first reaction was to say yes, because I didn't want to miss the opportunity, but after the reality of being in a deep, dark place hit me, I asked myself how I would be able to write. The only way I could do it was to set myself small goals of writing so many pages per day.

I am pleased to say that, as you can see, I accomplished what I set out to do. It may be interesting to write another book when I am in a manic state, so that we are able to compare the two.

Challenging Negative Thoughts

One of the most difficult aspects of depression is coping with the negative thoughts that happen moment to moment.

In 2004, when I split up with my long-term partner, I felt very guilty for staying with him so long and for taking the children away from their father. I also felt guilty about exposing the children to the negative effects of his heavy drinking.

The first line of treatment offered to me by my mental health care team was cognitive behavioural therapy (CBT), which is now widely used as a frontline treatment in the National Health Service (NHS) for treating depression.

CBT is a way of talking about how you think about yourself, the world, and other people and how what you do affects your thoughts and feelings. CBT can help you change how you think (cognitive) and what you do (behaviour). These changes can help you feel better. It focuses on the here and now, problems, and difficulties. It looks at ways to improve your mind.

CBT proved quite useful, as my therapist started to focus on the language I was using and pointed out to me how negative it was. She helped me turn around the way I used language, from negative to positive, so my cup was half-full and not half-empty.

Depression leads you to focus on the bleak aspects of life, so death is always nearby during these moments. I contemplated taking my life twice during this time. Suicidal thoughts were inextricably linked to the depression; without it, I would never consider such an act—I have my children and would never willingly want to leave them.

Suicidal thoughts are very common, and many people would never follow through even though they have these negative thoughts. Doctors worry more if you have actually made a plan to kill yourself, for example by an overdose, because the more concrete the thoughts of follow-through, the more likely you are to take action.

In my view, depression is a very selfish illness. It makes you self-centred and doesn't give you the opportunity to engage in other people's lives. There is more chance that the person who is depressed will find themselves having a chat in their own head rather than engaging with other people.

During my five-month depression, my mental health care team encouraged me to go out regularly on Fridays with Kay and my friend Karen. We went to a local pub in Sevenoaks called The Black Boy. It was quite interesting how I would not speak to any of the new people we would meet, but would sit quietly. All I could hear was the negative voice in my head, and I had a complete lack of confidence in having anything positive to say. Every time I returned from an evening at The Black Boy, I would announce that I was not going out to the pub the next Friday. Then Friday night would come round and both Kay and Karen would be insistent, and I would try once again.

Initially, I was worried that everyone could tell I was depressed because of my negative body language; I felt that my lack of conversation was a real giveaway. But every week I would turn up at The Black Boy, and each week I found it got easier. I believe that structure has really helped me manage the depression.

Managing Depression

People often ask me whether I think you can take an active role in managing and reducing your depression. I answer a very big yes to this question. We know that bipolar depression is clinical, so no matter what you do the depression will be there. It is very important that you take whatever medication you are prescribed in order to help alleviate the depression.

For me one of the important factors in managing my depression is to try and change my environment as much as possible. By this I mean visiting those insistent friends and family or going on the weekend breaks with them that they insist you take.

Based on my own experience, I believe that the more you mix with people the better it is, as it makes you participate in life activities. It is also good, as cited earlier, to try to hold on to as many activities as possible that give you a structure, such as work or regular meetings, classes etc. This is often the first thing to go as people feel they cannot cope, but I believe that it should be considered the last.

We know that the mental well-being of someone is dependent on physical well-being. When I am depressed, it is really important that I try to walk or swim. This is not always possible, as the depression gets a hold and I start to stay in bed 15 hours a day. To challenge the negative thoughts and not stay in bed all day takes real willpower. You have to stay focused and have a structure to your day, so that you have reasons for getting out of bed. It also is important that you have family and friends who insist you get up and go out and change your environment.

I can't repeat enough how important it is to try to work through depression. It may be that you work fewer hours or just a couple of days a week. Even if it is just a short amount of time, this gives structure and focus to your life in an ongoing way.

So, to summarize, here are suggestions that have helped me cope with major depression:

- Structure to the day;
- Remaining in work, if possible;
- Changing your environment;
- Taking prescribed medication;
- Keeping appointments with medical professionals;
- Socializing with friends and family;
- Eating sensibly and following a healthy eating plan;
- Exercise, such as walking, swimming, gym, and other forms of aerobic exercise;
- Complementary medicines.

Talking Heads

CHAPTER THREE

A *Personal Journey into a Psychiatric Ward*

During my eight years with this illness I have had five manic episodes and two major depressions. I would like to give you an inside look at the journey I took with mania in 2009.

In May of that year, if you had looked at me you may have believed that I was mentally fine. On the surface, I was able to give off an image of serenity; in fact, beneath the surface, I was paddling away furiously to stay afloat. No one was aware of the state I was in. Not my social worker nor my family and friends. I managed to put a screen around me so no one could really see what was happening.

As far back as January 2009, I was very aware that the business I had built up and run for the past 20 years was in decline. My company, Up Front, was a training company specializing in teaching individuals and groups how to communicate effectively, be it selling, presenting concepts, or influencing the boss for a pay rise. My sister Kay and I worked together at the company, but promises of work from even the most reliable clients were not being met due to the credit crunch. To my dismay, six key clients all cancelled contracts within three months of each other.

I decided to keep the company open another two months to see if Kay and I could change the hand of fate. We worked all hours and put every ounce of creativity into the company, to no avail. After banging our heads against a brick wall, or you could say fishing in the wrong waters, Up Front went bust in March 2009.

When I made the decision to close Up Front, my company and personal debts were in the region of £55,000. As you can imagine, it was a very painful experience to lose my company after two decades. Moreover, I had grown to rely on Kay to spot signs of mania in me. Now that she was no longer going to be working with me every day, I remember feeling very nervous and concerned.

The financial pressure to keep a roof over my family's head as a single mother began to really take its toll. I started to show signs of incipient mania, and in March, key indicators of mania, as defined by my medical team, started to kick in.

Key indicators are unique to each individual. In me, they included:

- **Painting at night.**
  Each night, I would paint about five paintings, in oils that were near masterpieces, according to friends and family. This affected my sleeping patterns, as I was awake all night.
- **Obsessively cleaning and throwing away articles in each room.**
  In each refuse bag I would throw in sugar, salt, and lemonade. The reason for this is I had started to feel a bad spirit around me, and anything white poured onto black or red things made sense to me.
- **Talking more about God, miracles, and heaven.**
  God became a real comfort at this time, and I started to speak to Mary, Jesus, and God himself.

My family and social worker knew I was running too fast, although in every conversation I had with them I had a very logical explanation for my behaviour. Nor were they aware of the extent of my bizarre actions. They noticed the build-up of black refuse sacks—"spring cleaning," I explained—but they did not know that inside the refuse sacks everything was covered in sugar, salt, and lemonade!!

It seemed my personal traumas were building. My eldest daughter, who was just 16 years old, was suffering from severe depression and had even contemplated taking her own life. Caring for her and seeing her pain definitely contributed to my manic episode.

Then, in early May, my mother's mental health issues were suddenly thrust into the spotlight. She is a lovely person but she suffers from obsessive compulsive disorder (OCD), schizophrenia, and dementia and is really difficult to care for. She does not accept that she is ill, which makes it a nightmare to try and help her.

My mother's own social worker had arranged a family meeting where we were all to discuss her ongoing needs. At this meeting, my mother became very agitated about being the focus of the discussion, feeling that we were all ganging up on her and trying to deprive her of her liberty. She became so aggressive with my stepfather that the mental health professionals at the meeting decided that my mother needed to be "sectioned."

In the UK, involuntary sectioning in a mental institution for a period of 28 days under the Mental Health Act of 1983 is permitted if someone is showing signs of a mental disorder and being a danger to themselves, in order for authorities to do a thorough assessment of a patient's needs. Generally, a patient can only be sectioned if two doctors and a social worker or a close relative of the patient believe it is necessary. One of these doctors is usually a psychiatrist. The other is often a doctor who knows the patient well.

My mother had been involuntarily committed in a mental institution five times before, and I did not want to see this happen again. I made an on-the-spot decision to offer my mother respite at my home for the weekend so that her health care team could take the time to consider the best living situation for her. I believed by removing my mother from the situation, it would allow things to calm down and she could avoid being institutionalized.

My sisters agreed with me, but were unable to offer to take her home due to their family commitments. They were both uneasy about me assuming the responsibility for our mother, but we saw no other option. After all, it was only for the weekend.

So I took my mother home with me. I wanted to make her feel at home, and I must have done a good job because whilst she was with me she asked if she could stay—not just for the weekend . . . but for life. My automatic answer was yes.

When my sisters heard what had transpired, they did all they could to dissuade me. But I was adamant that my mother was going nowhere; she was going to stay with my children and me.

Whilst my mother was at my house, I began showing other key indicators of mania. My spending patterns changed, and I bought silk sheets, expensive kitchenware, clothes for my mother, all to make her feel at home. I cared for my mother for three weeks, 24 hours a day. I was completely exhausted. On the positive side, not thinking about my own illness allowed me to forget for once that I had bipolar disorder. In reality, though, that was not the best thing to do.

I was aware that the signs of mania had already begun to show themselves—signs such as my negative obsession with anything red and black. Unfortunately, awareness was not enough, and I did not confront the situation nor did I ask for help as the mania began to take control.

Things continued to get stranger. My mother kept saying that she could hear the call of a fox and would ask me to go outside and investigate. Yet each time I did so, I would come back and tell her there was no fox there. But nothing would keep her calm, and she kept making reference to the red fox and how it was a bad spirit. It was at this point that she told me that she felt that the red fox had entered the house.

This now entered my own psyche. In my own mind, the red fox had become the devil after my youngest son.

One Saturday in late spring, I was at home entertaining my daughter and her two friends. We had one drink, then another, then another, and eventually, it turned into a very late night. During the course of the night, I started to throw away everything that had black or red associated with it. I threw away sunglasses, candles, shoes, clothes—all in the fight to get rid of the red fox. I was building up to a volcanic eruption and the alcohol was fuelling it. I removed all bed coverings from my family's beds and left them to sleep in white duvets, as I believed this would protect them from the red fox.

As the night progressed, I became very frightened, and as the fear heightened I started to drink vodka shots, believing that this white spirit would protect me. I followed this with three bottles of white wine. My eldest daughter was now starting to worry; she knows the signs of mania.

I asked my son if I could destroy his red fox furry toy. He wanted to be able to help me and said that I could. I then asked him to play a game of tug-of-war with the red fox. The stomach of the red fox ripped, and we pulled out the white stuffing from the fox. I felt that I had to get rid of the red fur. I threw it as far as I could onto an old bonfire site, leaving only the white stuffing, which in my mind would protect us.

Once the fox had been destroyed I collapsed on the sofa and managed to sleep for a short while. The night of complete mania lasted until 5.30 a.m. I was completely out of it, believing totally that Satan had entered the house and was after my youngest son. The only reason I fell asleep was because I was exhausted and had no energy left to deal with the devil.

The following morning my daughter called Kay to come and assess the situation, as she had been so worried by my behaviour the night before. Kay realized I was very unwell and called the doctors to get me an assessment to see if I needed to be admitted to hospital. A doctor arrived within 20 minutes and decided that it was best I was admitted. He asked many questions and realized how unwell I was. He wanted me to go to Little Brook Hospital in Dartford, where I had been in 2004 for an assessment.

I agreed to go, and my sister and daughter drove me to the hospital. This saved an ambulance coming to the house. I am very fortunate to have neighbours who know I have bipolar disorder and look out for me, but I decided to keep the situation under wraps for the moment.

When we arrived at Little Brook we were shown to a waiting room where we met Boo, a male nurse. My mania was set off just by hearing his name. "Boo," I kept shouting. Nobody laughed.

The psychiatrist I eventually saw was a young woman wearing black shoes. I remember this vividly because I was so set against anything black or red. I recall telling her how uncomfortable her shoes made me feel, and she was kind enough to take them off so that I would feel more settled.

There was a black phone on the psychiatrist's desk. This became another distraction because I then found myself focusing on the fact that this would be a means for the devil to make contact. I remember that I kept banging the phone. Why couldn't they realize how dangerous this was?

In addition, we had taken bottles of water with us to the hospital, and I remember that I kept pouring the water over myself. My sister and daughter didn't understand that I was trying to cleanse myself and get rid of the devil—they were even more shocked when I poured the water over them!!

As you can imagine, the doctors realized just how ill I was and made arrangements for me to be admitted to the psychiatric ward.

From what happened to me on this occasion, here are the conclusions I reached:

- When experiencing mania everything that happens—for example, the red fox becoming the devil—is *real* to that person at the time.
- Experiencing the devil coming for my son was very alarming and frightening. No one could have convinced me at the time that what I was experiencing was not real.
- There is an opportunity when you first go into mania to ask for help. At that point, you retain the ability to be aware of your bizarre behaviour, but the longer you leave it the sooner the illness takes over.
- Key indicators will always show before a manic attack. It is very important that you and your loved ones and doctors are all aware of what your particular key indicators are and watch for them.
- A manic episode triggers out-of-control behaviour, which is a very frightening experience. On the positive side, you *will* come down from this phase and normality will be restored.

Life on a Psychiatric Ward

To date, I have been on a psychiatric ward three times, and I am sure that there will be occasions in the future, too. Key to understanding bipolar is knowing that life on a psychiatric ward is part of the journey.

My first stay in a mental hospital was in 1991. I was living in London and the year before, my father had died of stomach cancer at the age of 52. I found I could not cope with the loss of him. Everything happened so fast—the time between my dad receiving his diagnosis and his death was a period of just six weeks.

I became very depressed and finally, even though it was a hard decision, I voluntarily admitted myself to hospital for treatment. I was actually turned away three times before being admitted, as the hospital staff didn't believe I needed help. Each time I returned, I explained that I lived in a tower block on the 15th floor and had this overwhelming feeling that I wanted to throw myself off. I was so desperate, they eventually agreed to take me in.

Because I had voluntarily admitted myself to hospital I was not initially "sectioned." But after six weeks on the psychiatric ward, I was so unwell that, even though I had voluntarily asked to be admitted, I kept trying to escape and at that point had to be sectioned for my own well-being.

In 1991, the hospital did not offer much in terms of treatment. Psychiatric patients stayed on the ward, highly medicated, and the approach was for time to be the healer. But in 2004, when I was admitted to Little Brook Hospital, I had a very different experience.

The first test is actually getting a place on the ward. You have to be extremely mentally unwell to be detained. The psychiatrist carried out her assessment by asking plenty of questions and observing my behaviour. I was unable to process simple information, my behaviour was erratic, I couldn't stop crying, and my smoking was out of control. As a result, I was booked into the hospital and onto the ward.

I was very fortunate to be given my own ensuite room, which I remember as being spotless. There were about 20 people on the ward, a mixture of males and females. This was quite scary because everyone was on medication to sedate them, although the tension on the ward was immense. Much of your time on the ward had to be used up by making sure you did not upset other people. It was quite intimidating most of the time.

The ward was run in a very orderly way: there was always a specific time and place for everything. As soon as I was allowed to get up, I would go out into the courtyard and smoke one cigarette after another. It was here that the patients would meet for company.

You had to work out what made each person tick. Cigarettes were a bargaining tool that you could use to get more perks from other patients. I remember one day having no hair shampoo and, since the hospital did not provide this, I offered a couple of cigarettes to a patient and, hey presto, I could have clean hair.

After the morning cigs, it was time for breakfast. This was a fight every morning, as each patient wanted to get to the table first. One thing about antipsychotic drugs is it makes you hungry all the time, so you become very obsessed with food, which can lead some patients to get very aggressive. Food was a major focus on the ward, and during all my stays on psychiatric wards, I have found the food to be really nutritious and plentiful.

After breakfast was ward rounds. Some of the patients would see the doctor, whilst others had no need. Seeing the doctor made the day go faster, and if you did not see the doctor that day, time could seem endless. The hospital offered occupational therapy during part of the day, where you could choose to attend one of the many classes on art, needlework, news night, crafts, hair and beauty, body and mind, and music therapy. I found myself drifting into all the classes at some point.

I was on strong antipsychotic medication, along with a mood stabilizer and sleeping tablets, when I was first admitted to hospital, so participation in any of the above was difficult. But as I moved into my second week on the psychiatric ward, I began to get bored. This is a really good sign, as it shows you are getting better and in need of stimulation.

Unfortunately, the art class lacked materials—only pencils were available, which suppressed my creativity as I wanted to paint in oils. The needlework class was not much better. It offered "stuffing a felt frog" for excitement. The best class for me was the hair and beauty class, where I got to receive a massage, have my nails painted, and get a haircut! These classes offered the chance to build stronger relationships with other patients. Remember: everyone is very ill on a psychiatric ward, and relationships can be built one day and destroyed the next due to the mental state of that person. Life on the wards was very unpredictable, so taking classes with each other was a bonding opportunity that in other circumstances may not have happened.

Lunchtime was the next big gathering for patients. Without fail there would be arguments—who would be sitting where and more importantly, who would be getting their food first? It always reminded me of feeding hungry animals at a zoo. We would have three nurses present at all times, serving food and controlling the mayhem.

After lunch you would normally get time with a nurse to talk about your day, which was quite comforting. This did not always happen; it depended on what was happening on the ward. If a crisis occurred, then the nurses would be dispatched to deal with this, and as a result, your time with them was shortened or did not happen.

The best part of the day was when visitors came. I loved my family coming to see me, although they have since told me how frightened they were coming into a place like that, with so many people unwell. But I was very focused on getting better at the time and did not think of them and whether they were frightened. All I thought about was seeing my three beautiful children and my sisters and close friends.

Life on the ward is nerve-wracking because all the patients are fragile and are on very strong medication, but I believe each time I have been on the ward it has been the best place for me. I have felt safe and know and trust the medical team will get me well again. I would much prefer to be cared for in hospital than at home. At home, I have three children to look after and am unable to care for them when I am so unwell. Thankfully, every time I have been seriously unwell, a stay in the hospital has been the only option. The staff there have never let me down.

CHAPTER FOUR

Family and Friends

As I related earlier, being diagnosed with a mental illness is very scary for everyone involved. It is also a very isolating illness, as loved ones who don't understand the bizarre behaviour can turn against you. This certainly happened to me.

My brother and the rest of my family were trying to deal with my mother, who was severely ill and in and out of mental hospitals. I, on the other hand, had always been successful running my own business and travelling the world, so no one believed that I needed help. I was expected to look after myself.

When I received my bipolar diagnosis in 2004, my brother came up to visit me in hospital. Since he found me able to speak coherently, he decided that I must be fine. His words to me were that he would not be up again as he could see that I was alright and a little rest would sort me out. My brother was in denial, and explaining my illness to him at that time was no use. He did not intend to break my heart in saying this, but nevertheless I did feel heartbroken by his words. His lack of understanding had a detrimental effect on my mental health. You would never be in a secure unit of a mental hospital unless you were very unwell. It was not my brother's fault; it was simply a lack of knowledge on his part about my illness. He was making decisions based on what he *thought* he saw.

My sisters' reactions to my illness were very different. They decided to read everything they could about bipolar disorder on the Internet (and there is a lot of information written on the subject, believe me!). By the time I got to speak to them they were feeling terrified by my diagnosis.

I explained simply that bipolar was a mood swing illness and the easiest way to think about it was that I could travel "high up the pole or fall low down the pole"—and neither place was a good place to be. The job of my medical team was to get me nicely placed in the middle.

I also explained that I believe the illness has fuelled my creativity. When I have been in a hypomanic state, I have been able to create my best works of art, come up with my best work ideas, and generally be intuitive. This has empowered me and made me who I am today— a successful woman raising her family single-handedly. I explained to my sisters that I would not give up my bipolar state, even if they found a cure. Bipolar is part of who I am.

The above explanation made sense to my sisters but did not cover psychosis, which terrified both of them. They could not believe that their intelligent sister, who ran her own company and mixed with all types of influential people, could at some point lose her mind and find herself channelling the Virgin Mary. (The Virgin Mary was not the only character I channelled whilst in psychosis—I've been the Goddess Athena, God, and the Archangel Gabriel, amongst others!) I found the best way of explaining psychosis was to involve my medical team in helping to explain more about it. So I invited my sisters to my Care Plan Approach (CPA) meeting, which is held roughly every six months, where speaking to my psychiatrist helped them better understand bipolar disorder.

When I have had to explain bipolar disorder to friends, I have had very different reactions. One very dear friend is anti the use of medication and has said to me on numerous occasions that I should put my medication in the bin. She really believes that this would be the best solution for me. She can see that the drugs are numbing my creativity, and as she is an artist and a writer herself she gets very frustrated.

This is not helpful advice, though. Taking medication is a constant challenge for me, even at the best of times. So often the little voice inside me says: *No more of this. You're okay. You don't need this medication any longer.* But experience has shown me that if I were to come off the drugs I would go into mania. I have tried it a few times, and each time I have gone into mania, and each time, the crisis team has managed to get me well again but has had to spend weeks trying to convince me that the medication is necessary.

I've got other friends who have been very understanding. They look out for me and let me know when my voice sounds pressured and whether I am running too fast. They have taken the time to understand the illness and are not frightened by it. They like me and see my bipolar disorder as my friend, not my foe.

One area that has been difficult is explaining bipolar disorder to a new boyfriend. It is surprising how little knowledge men seem to have on the subject of bipolar disorder; nor do they seem to want to take it on board when I discuss it with them. In general, I have found men shy away from mental health issues. This is a great shame, because there are long periods when you feel really well despite the disease. In most cases, I believe the best way to understand bipolar is to bring in the medical team to help explain the situation.

Inclusion – Meet the Health Professionals

It is essential to have an understanding family doctor (GP) who relates to bipolar disorder. You need to be able to go and speak to him or her and adjust your medication when needed. It is important to be able to express how you are feeling and get proper advice and direction. Often, your family doctor is the first person involved in your case.

I have been very lucky with my GP. He has a brother with the same illness and always knows when I am heading towards mania, as I ask him things like, "Are you Father Christmas and will you bring me presents?" Asking this question in the middle of June is a real giveaway! I trust my GP and value his opinion. If he feels I need more drugs, or that I need to visit the Community Mental Health Team (CMHT) who manage my mental health care, I will generally follow his advice.

Community Mental Health Team (CMHT)

In the UK, if a family doctor has concerns about someone's mental health, he or she refers the patient to the CMHT, a team made up of NHS psychologists, occupational behavioural therapists, support workers, social workers, and other health care professionals. Team members come up with an action plan to manage the patient's mental health needs. If you are a UK resident, have bipolar disorder, and have had hospital treatment, you would probably be managed by the CMHT.

I find CMHT meetings very useful. This is the time I invite family members along to understand how I am feeling and express where I am on the pole. To date, my two sisters, Kay and Jill, and my daughters, Megan and Brooke, have come to the meetings to express their feelings about how I am coping. It is amazing how insightful they can be about my illness.

If I am in a hypomanic state, my self-confidence is often massive and I may not realize that I am getting close to mania. It is the knowledge loved ones have accrued about bipolar disorder that then gives them the skills to articulate any problems to the mental health professionals in charge of my care. Without these meetings, my bipolar disorder could go undetected, leading to mania or severe depression.

Psychiatrist

Your psychiatrist is in charge of your medication and your overall well-being. Finding a psychiatrist who understands you and listens to your desires is fundamental in helping to keep you well.

I have had three different psychiatrists since 2004. The first psychiatrist was someone who did things by the book and never really listened to my needs. For example, I tried to explain on many occasions that the drugs I was on—risperidel and lithium—were making me fat; I had gone from a UK size 10 to a UK size 18 in two years. But my psychiatrist could not see that the effort to keep me mentally well was having a negative effect on my physical health. He did nothing to help me in this regard, and I was only too pleased when he left.

My second psychiatrist was very different. He was willing to listen and understood that putting on weight was bad for my state of mind. He changed my antipsychotic drug straight away, putting me on Seroquel XL, which I too believed at the time would help my situation. But as time went on, I put on even more weight and realized that my antipsychotic drug was not helping me at all. I got so depressed I needed to go on an antidepressant. But that drug led to mania a couple of months afterwards. This yoyo effect is quite common, and it is the reason why psychiatrists only prescribe antidepressants as a last resort. The antidepressants increase the serotonin levels in the brain and can overshoot; it is this imbalance that can lead to mania.

My current psychiatrist is someone who is willing to take risks and work with me. The first thing she did was changing my antipsychotic medication from Seroquel XL to Ariprazole. This change was not seamless. It required a psychiatrist who was willing to listen to me, experiment with the dosage of the drug, and not to give up when things were not quite right. After a couple of months of trial and error, we have found the correct dosage and I continue to do well on Ariprazole. My weight is gradually coming down with this new medication, and I am in a much better place.

I've recently suffered an attack of low bipolar, although I do not associate this with being on Ariprazole. I am currently being treated with an antidepressant, which is a risk for the reasons mentioned above, but one I believe worth taking. My current psychiatrist is fully aware of the problems I had on antidepressants in the past and started me on a very low dose of Sertraline (50mg), increasing for a short while to 100mg, and then reducing back down to 50mg.

Care Coordinator (Social Worker):

In the UK, the role of the care coordinator is fundamental to the well-being of the bipolar patient (who, in official NHS language, is called the Service User). The care coordinator will often be a social worker, and it is this person's job to see you on a regular basis. This could be once a week or once a month, whatever is required.

It is the care coordinator's responsibility to liaise between the mental health professionals and the patient, look out for key indicators of incipient mania, speak to family, and call emergency meetings with the psychiatrist, if necessary, amongst other duties.

I have had three care coordinators, and they have all been very different. My first care coordinator, a woman I will call Louise, was very nice but not strong enough to stand up to me. I needed someone who would challenge me and offer advice when I was going into a manic state, but Louise was unable to recognize my key indicators. I have a very open, bubbly personality, and the fact that I have a large persona and have been professionally very successful blindsided her into missing my need for medical intervention. Also lacking in this relationship was any sense of connection between us. I needed her to share stories about her life and me to share information about mine. Because we could not do that, a close bond was not able to form. Fortunately, you can ask to change your care coordinator. It is essential that the personality mix is right.

My second care coordinator was amazing. Gina understood my every move. She was always one step ahead. I remember one really difficult situation that she had to deal with. I was in hospital and my two sisters were finding it nearly impossible to look after me, my mother with her own mental health issues, and their own families. It was Gina who approached me about my mother going into care. This was a delicate situation, and Gina handled it perfectly. She found the confidence to discuss this with me, which my two sisters could not, because as I mentioned earlier, I was totally against my mother being institutionalized.

Gina also was instrumental in helping me sort out my financial situation at the time. Whilst in hospital I had gone to the Advocacy Team, a team that helps patients manage their finances, but due to a lack of staff they were unable to offer assistance. This left me feeling very vulnerable, as my financial pressures were huge. Gina took it upon herself to write letters to the electricity board, the gas board, my mortgage company, and other creditors, informing them that I was in hospital and would need time to pay their bills when I came out of hospital. This was a great help at the time, as I was too unwell to administer my affairs and unable to cope with the stress this produced. This just shows how great she was.

My third care coordinator, Kate, is also wonderful. My relationship with her is still fairly new. We have a very good relationship and understand one another. Kate has a special gift of being able to listen, understand, and know which health professional will be best able to help. Each time there has been a challenge I have had to face (normally to do with the financial stress I have found myself in over the course of the last few years), like Gina before her, Kate has been able to help by writing letters to creditors. Currently, Kate visits me once a week to keep me on track and monitor my well-being.

The Crisis Team

The NHS Crisis Team includes doctors, social workers, and psychiatrists and exists to keep you out of hospital, where possible. When you are in crisis, the care coordinator calls the crisis team, and the team members come to your home. To do its job, the crisis team requires that the bipolar patient be open and honest about the way he or she feels and be willing to cooperate. I have called upon the crisis team five times in eight years. That just shows you how often I go into mania or depression.

When you are in crisis, the crisis team visits your home every day and makes sure that you take your medication. When you are in a manic state, the crisis team spends time speaking to you in an effort to help you face reality. On the other side of the coin, when you are in a depressive state, the team talks to you and helps you focus on the positives of each day.

I would recommend drawing on the expertise of the crisis team in order to stay out of hospital. When I have gone into psychosis, personally I find that hospitalization is best for me for the first few days as I have children at home and I feel that I can't care for them properly whilst I am in a psychotic state. When I am free from the psychosis and out of hospital, it is important once again that I work closely with the crisis team in order to get well.

Family and Friends' Reactions
to Bipolar Disorder

Bipolar disorder is an illness that affects everyone around you. It is important to take their feelings into consideration. Each person will have a different reaction and coping strategy. When I spoke to my family and friends these are the different reactions I got.

Brooke, my 14-year-old daughter

When you are in a depressed mood, Mum, I can't stop worrying about you. I always want to make sure you take your tablets because I don't want you to go into hospital. I don't like to see you down and depressed because it makes me down and depressed. It is scary seeing you when you are high. I don't know what you are going to do next. You change completely and it freaks me out.

Zac, my 11-year-old son

It is fine, Mum. Not worrying, perfectly fine. Nothing to worry about. You are the perfect mother who can handle herself.

Oh, to be so young!!

Megan, my eldest daughter

Being the eldest, I feel responsible for looking out for your key indicators. I know I have to make sure you take your medication because without it you will definitely go into mania. I wouldn't change you for the world, though. Don't ever lose your personality, Mum. I love you just the way you are.

Kay, my eldest sister

It is worrying, I don't stop worrying and looking out for you. Life with you has always been interesting. As I've always said, Lynn is either flying up high or down below. In the middle with the rest of the world is not a place that suits you. Since [your] being diagnosed with bipolar, it has helped me better understand your personality over the years. It has not been an easy journey, but it has never been boring.

You have always been the sister who creates — firstly your business, then your art, and now your book. It has been quite difficult for my family to understand when you have a manic episode that you are unwell, because they normally see you when you are high and look to be functioning on all levels. None of us likes to see you in depression, and we all try to keep you as buoyant as possible. I do, however, realize with you that there can be no light without the dark. We just like to keep the dark as short as possible.

Jill, sister

Well, you would think that all the help in the world was at hand when your sister has bipolar. What is bipolar, I asked myself? Lots of different theories have been put forward, but mainly manic depression keeps cropping up. Then I asked myself, depression??? Well, nearly all the times you have had an episode of bipolar, it has always been when you are very, very high. You have always been driven, dynamic, creative, slightly eccentric (many different hats in the 80s rings a few bells!). Always an inspiration to so many in your work, family, and friends.

When you become high, you certainly do things to the extreme. Any normal person would question, "What the hell is she doing?" but you go on an adrenaline rush like no other. My children and I have come to understand the illness a lot more over the years — it has, however, taken an inordinate length of time for my husband to realize that you have an illness.

My daughter Katie is very close to you and is always asking regularly how you are? Katie is always there to support me through your episodes, too, as they have had detrimental effects on myself and my sister Kay. We have gone into meltdown ourselves, with the sheer exhaustion of dealing with each situation as it occurs, looking after your children, and also trying to look after our own families whilst your episodes are occurring.

Strangely enough, when your most recent episode occurred, you went into a depression instead of a high. Ooohh, I really hated to see you so down. Everyone said that they were really concerned for you, as it lasted for approximately five months. Even my husband said, "God, Lynn really isn't well." Oh well, it has only taken him approximately eight years to realize how unwell you can become — but that's men for you!!

I love you unconditionally, high or low — as we should all love our family members. And, yes, we have had some "hairy" times throughout your time with bipolar, but I will always be there for you, as you have always been there for me. Because you know what? That's what sisters are for!!!

Barbara Harrison, best friend:

Bipolar? That's a difficult one, because to me you are Hodges, and you have always been the same. In hindsight, you have obviously always been bipolar since we have known each other; it just didn't have a name then. I love the fact that it allows your creativity to flow, that when you are up you are always such good fun, with great energy levels and hugely inspiring from a business point of view. I also love to see you having such fun, even when it's slightly over the top, slightly embarrassing (taking your clothes off in public) now and again, but never, ever dull.

But it worries me a lot when you come down, and I hate hearing you when you are low, knowing that I can't do anything to help and it is a matter of time or medication. It's hard to watch from the outside. I worry whether your medical team are looking after you okay, although I know that you have a good understanding and take responsibility for, and control of, your condition. I am reassured that your sisters are close and can keep an eye on you, and the kids are great and seem to cope with it well. But you are a worry.

I think you cope amazingly with it, with three children and a home to run on your own, a business that has gone under, and having to deal with the aftermath of that and the financial stress. Yet you're still out there doing it, coming up with ideas, never stopping or giving in (unless you really can't do it). [You are doing] more than most people would manage, but then you're a fighter. I wouldn't change you for the world, but I would take away the depression for you if I could.

As you can hear, the people who love you the most worry the most. It's important to remember how much concern they do have for you. I don't actually worry about my illness. I accept it for what it is—although I do get frustrated from time to time, never knowing from what end of the pole I will swing.

I find it hardest to cope with the depression that comes with bipolar. I've recently had my darkest depression, one where I have been unable to get out of bed. Normal activities like driving have been too much for me. My anxiety levels have been so high I have been unable to drive long distances or to places I haven't been before. My doctor tried treating the depression with an antidepressant, but as I mentioned earlier, this can sometimes shoot you into mania, so it is a risk. It just means that we have to take things slowly and try not to rush. I am now out of the depression, and life is slowly beginning to move from black and white to colour. I am smiling once again.

CHAPTER FIVE

Positive Images

I always remember that before I was diagnosed with a mental illness I was a whole person. People asked me what I did, what my interests were. I was a person who used her creative mind with freedom.

Everyone who knows me understands that I use the creative, right side of my brain much more than my logical left. My creative side is far superior to my logical side. This was accepted in my circle of friends and with my work colleagues. I found I could produce excellent results at work, and my friends enjoyed having a whacky mate.

The moment I found out I had bipolar disorder life was very different. First the mental health team wanted to dampen everything with antipsychotic drugs, leaving only the left side of the brain in operation. I often wonder about what would happen if Mozart was alive today and was damped down by antipsychotics. Would he still be a genius or would he be merely mediocre?

The crazy thing is that we are all made up of so many facets. Having a mental illness is only part of someone's character. I don't let someone know I'm bipolar unless I am asked. This way, I can continue my life without prejudice. Many times, bipolar will come up in conversation, and I will admit straight away that I have the illness. I don't think it's anything to be embarrassed about, but it's often less complicated not to mention it.

I have found it difficult on the job market if I reveal I have a mental illness. Whether it's going for high-powered positions in Human Resources or a job as a waitress in a café, the reaction is the same if I dare to mention bipolar. Every employer who has interviewed me has seemed to have a very limited view of the illness. We know by law that everyone should be treated the same, but in reality this is not always the case, and hasn't been for me.

Having a mental illness does take up a lot of time, it's true, because you have to attend CPA meetings with your family, care coordinator, and psychiatrist. You also have to be available to see your care coordinator independently on a regular basis. And you have to take medication for the rest of your life.

It is hard to ignore the fact that you are mentally unwell. It never seems to go away. This cycle of events does nothing to make you feel better; in fact, it can make you feel worse about yourself, and you can become depressed. Often I feel like a hamster in a cage—constantly going round on the wheel.

I have found the best way to come to terms with my mental illness is to build up all the other aspects of my life and to try to become as successful as possible. I had been a businesswoman for 22 years, teaching people how to communicate with impact. When I think of that time, I know that my bipolar was very much part of me. I don't think I could have run my company without the mix of bipolar characteristics. To work with people at the top of industry, you had to be pretty wacky, to say the least.

I remember one bipolar moment when I was running Up Front. I had just started my business, and we were in the first year of trading. Money was very tight. We had delivered training for an advertising agency and they had not paid their invoice. The invoice was now 60 days overdue, and we could not afford to wait a day longer for payment. I went into reception at the agency and literally sang for my money. *I've delivered the goods, so pay for your goods. I want my money now. Don't let me down. I've delivered the goods, so pay for your goods right now.* And so on.

Not surprisingly, the receptionist just wanted me to leave, although she did appreciate my humour. I gave her the invoice, and she called her boss, explaining that there was a woman in reception singing for her money. I must say the cheque was down in reception quicker than a wink. It was obvious that they wanted me out of there, as they did not want me bothering their clients.

I remember another time, when I was waiting in the reception of a new client. Most people would be seated, waiting respectfully for the opportunity to meet with a potential client. This may have been how most people greeted clients, but I found myself lying on the floor, practising breathing techniques. When the client came out, I asked if he wanted to join me on the floor, so we could relax prior to the meeting. It was amazing how many people actually joined me on the floor!

And the last story I'll share with you is the day I asked a client to be a fried egg. We were working on her public speaking skills, and I wanted her to get more energy into her work. No matter how I phrased my suggestions about increasing the energy, she could not grasp the fact that she lacked it. But the moment she did what I asked and experienced herself being a fried egg (wobbling around in a frying pan creating movement), she was able to relate to energy and was able to be successful in her public speaking.

For a mental disorder to be just a part of you and not take over as the whole thing, it is important to work on all the other areas of your life. The areas that I focus on are being a single mum bringing up three beautiful children. Any parent will know how much time and energy is needed for this role. As a parent, I am entertainer, counsellor, best friend, taxi driver… and that's just for starters. It is a relentless job, but one with so many benefits.

The great joy for me is that my children see more than the bipolar. My children see me as a full-time mother, businesswoman, artist, and writer. They know when bipolar is about, and they worry, as all children would. Although my 11-year-old says he doesn't worry, I think he does really and is just putting on a brave face.

As a professional artist, I find working with oils a great way of expressing my moods. My work shows whether I am in hypomania, mania, or depression. Painting often helps me to change from one mood to another.

Since you are holding a book in your hands, you know too that I like to write. Writing for me is a way of escaping into another world, away from the children, away from everyday living.

Tips on Finding Positive Role Models

When people talk about finding a positive role model they normally mean looking at the public arena and finding an individual who they think represents them.

People with bipolar know that there are people in the public eye with bipolar who we can look up to, such as Stephen Fry, Ruby Wax, amongst others. But do these public figures really help us cope with bipolar in our own daily lives? I have to say that, for me, the answer is no. I need more tangible help, more tangible results. What I need to have in my life are strong people who are bipolar and family and friends who understand the illness. Having these people in my life, rather than looking to the public arena, is where I find my positive role models.

I have found great solace in being part of the Success Group, run by Kent County Council. This group was brought together so that members could tell their story to health professionals. All the members of the group suffer from mental illness or are carers for the mentally ill. Being part of a group with like-minded individuals gives you the opportunity to speak frankly about your illness. It is also good to get feedback from others about what they are experiencing.

For example, some people may have experienced taking certain medication and found that the side effects were such that they did not take it again. This is invaluable information if you are considering going on that particular medication. It is also good to hear stories about individual forms of mania and depression and to realize that you are not alone.

I always remember hearing about a man who had decided to go to his local pub and whilst he was there he saw all the people at the bar as warriors. He turned on them, using his hands as pistols, and basically shot up the bar. Obviously no one was hurt, but everyone was very nervous! The man then left the pub and made his way to the beach down the road. He believed that the war was still on, thought that he saw a boat out at sea, stripped naked, and went running down the beach. A member of the public called the police, and he was captured and sectioned.

For some, sharing stories in a group like this will be refreshing; others will find having someone in the public eye offers a better role model. Whatever works for you is fine. I find it better if I can speak to a person as well as see the individual.

I also think that role models can come in different guises. My young son is a role model to me. He has such a fresh approach in dealing with my behaviour. If I am becoming high, he says, "Mum, you are heading towards Pluto. Have you taken your pills?" When I am depressed, he says, "Lie there, if you need to, Mum, but you're missing a great day."

My daughters, Megan and Brooke, keep me on the straight and narrow and are both confident at spotting key indicators and alerting my mental health team. I am so happy to have them in my life.

Another role model for me is my mother. Although she is mentally ill, she is still able to be very clear with her message. She constantly reminds me that I am talented and that bipolar goes hand in hand with creativity. She gives me confidence that bipolar is just part of me—not the whole of who I am. She constantly reminds me of my talents. That is what a role model should do in my opinion.

My sister Kay is another role model. She constantly reminds me that I am a great mother and a very talented businesswoman. She builds my ego, giving me confidence that I am more than my illness.

My sister Jill tries to keep me going when all else has failed. She is great at rallying me and really helpful at getting me out of a depression.

Last but not least, my best friends Barbara, Sally, Linda, and Karen are role models for me. Barbara is always on the end of the telephone, willing to listen to my babble. Sally is on the Internet, listening to my news. And Linda and Karen are there, face-to-face, popping round for a cup of tea or a glass of wine, checking all is fine. I don't know what I would do without these people in my life.

Exercises to Increase Your Confidence and Positive Image

When you live with bipolar disorder, many times you will find that you lose confidence and are unable to keep up a positive exterior. The reasons for this will vary for everyone, but when I have spoken to other people who use mental health services about this, many have explained that, because at some point they have lost capacity, they feel very vulnerable.

'Losing capacity' means not being able to make decisions on your own behalf. Often when you go into mania, psychosis will be part of the experience and you won't be in a world of reality, therefore your capacity will be affected. After you have lost capacity and heard about your bizarre behaviour from family and friends, there is bound to be an impact on your confidence and personal image. It's the same at the other end of the manic spectrum when you are in depression, unable to get out of bed and operate.

Exercises that work for me in helping to restore capacity (several based on cognitive behavioural therapy, or CBT) are as follows:

Positive Self-Talk and Affirmations

When we feel depressed, the language we use is often very negative, and it is hard to find positive solutions to our negative thoughts. This situation is helped by positive self-talk. Affirmations allow you to take a phrase and memorize it, look in the mirror, and start to believe it.

An example of an affirmation might be: *I am very beautiful. I am very powerful. And everybody loves me.*

When you first say these words to the mirror, you will not believe it because you are feeling so down. The key to success here is to repeat the self-talk exercise several times a day. Over time, we start to believe what we say and think. The phrase you use can be completely up to you but must not contain any negative words. This is a very positive exercise. Here is an example of an affirmation I use:

- I am able to achieve all that I want to.
- I am interesting and intelligent.
- All I work for will be achieved.
- I am an excellent mother.
- I am a creator and believe in my ideas.
- I am caring and loving and sexy.
- I am worthy of great things.

What is important is you put together an affirmation that starts with "I." Each line needs to be positive. It is also important to write an affirmation that encompasses your whole life. Using an affirmation purely based around work is not as powerful as addressing everything. I say this every morning and every evening to the mirror. Looking at yourself whilst saying it is more powerful.

Visualization

Visualization is another very powerful tool. Often when we are depressed we feel fearful about everything. One small job is a huge feat. As we know, the mind is extremely powerful, and we can use the mind to visualize positive outcomes.

To do this exercise, make time to be alone, away from family and friends. You will only need 5–10 minutes, but you need to do the exercises consistently. Take a deep breath and visualize successful people, places, and abilities. This will help you feel more confident. It is important to tune into your five senses—hearing, taste, sight, touch, and smell. The more you can bring these into the visualization, the more your confidence will grow and will lead to a positive outcome. The following exercise engages your creativity and increases your ability to visualize successfully.

EXERCISE: **Visualizing an Object**
For this visualization you will need about 15 minutes. First find yourself a place where you can sit quietly and will not be disturbed.

- Breathe in, listening to your breath, and then breathe out again. Repeat this several times. This will have a calming effect and help you focus.
- Once you are prepared, focus your mind on a simple object, for example an orange. See the object in its full glory, the colour, the texture, the size and shape. As you see the orange, breathe in and out deeply to help keep you focussed.
- Now that you can see the orange, see if you can also smell it. Peel the orange back, count the segments; then split the orange open and see what you can smell. Breathe in deeply and exhale several times.
- Now taste the orange, how succulent is it? Or is it dry with no juice? What does the flesh of the orange taste like? Use your imagination to see, smell and taste the orange fully.
- Then breathe in for three counts, and out for five counts. Bring your awareness back into the room and open your eyes again.

Breathing and Relaxation

Breathing correctly gives you great power and confidence. We all breathe naturally, but learning how to breathe deeply is very therapeutic and will give you confidence.

There are many useful breathing techniques. Here is one. First, exhale fully, then breathe in through the nose and hold to a count of three, then exhale on a count of ten. Practising this for several minutes during the course of the day really helps you to feel grounded. To move on to the next stage you breathe in for three and exhale with an *Ah* sound to the count of ten. Learning to control the breath gives you a sense of empowerment.

EXERCISE: **Alternate Nostril Breathing**

This exercise has the power to balance and relax the body and also balance both hemispheres of the brain.

There are many ways to breathe to help you relax, though nothing is quite as good as the Alternate Nostril Breathing.

- Start the exercise by placing thumb and index finger over your nostrils (lightly).
- First gently press your left nostril down with your thumb releasing your index finger. Breathe in and hold your breath. Put your left index finger on your right nostril releasing your thumb and breathe out.
- Place your thumb on your left nostril again and press gently down releasing your index finger. Breathe in and hold your breath.
- Then release the thumb over your left nostril and breathe out again while gently placing your index finger over the right nostril.
- Repeat the exercise ten times.
- When you have completed the exercise take three deep breaths and relax.

Compliment yourself

To feel confident we need to hear positive feedback. The question is, why don't we pay *ourselves* compliments? If we simply focus our attention on what is good about ourselves, this would help us feel more confident. How often do you really compliment yourself? Praise yourself every day. It does not matter how small the praise. For example, if you have answered letters that needed a reply, praise yourself. If you have booked appointments for your children, give yourself a pat on the back. These are only small things, but small things add up to big things, and before we know it we are feeling good about ourselves.

Write in a notebook

I find writing things down in a notebook or journal really helpful. What I write in the notebook needs to be positive and reflect good aspects of my personality. I like to write things down because I can read over them and remind myself of my strengths.

Positive mood

It has been documented that one of the most powerful exercises we can do for our brain is to be thankful or grateful; it shifts the brain to a positive mood and creates health.

Goals

When you are depressed it is really difficult to come to terms with goals. It is enough to get out of bed. In short, that could be a goal and achieving getting out of bed is amazing. Small steps like making a cup of tea or going for a walk are all achievements when faced with the black cloud of depression. As time moves on, you can set yourself bigger goals and watch yourself achieve them. Remember: Small achievements mean greater self-worth.

Change your body language

When you are depressed, your body language naturally leans in and your arms will often be crossed in front of you. An easy physical exercise that you could do in combination with conscious breathing in/out would be the following:

EXERCISE: **Body-supported Breathing**

- Raise your arms high above your head and breathe in deeply. Then let the breath out whilst lowering the arms naturally in front of your body towards the ground. Let their weight pull you over, so that your body collapses to the floor. Stay in this position for several minutes and gently stretch the body out.
- Repeat several times. You will feel more confident and physically much taller.

Eye Contact

One of the first things that goes when you are depressed is eye contact. Engaging with others feels near impossible. I find the following exercise a useful way of counteracting this:

EXERCISE: **Eye Contact**

- Find yourself a quiet space where you will be undisturbed. Then take a mirror and looking into it, practise holding eye contact with your own image for five seconds.
- Place the mirror down and breathe deeply for some moments.
- Pick up the mirror again and now try and hold eye contact with your image for ten seconds.
- Continue this exercise until you are able to hold eye contact for 30 seconds or longer.

Once you have achieved the above it is good to go out and practise eye contact with other people, e.g. when talking to a shop assistant, with a colleague at work, or a friend.

These are just some of the exercises I use to help keep me well. It is true that when I am in the depths of depression it is hard to do any of the above, but I try my best. I know what is good for me and what will help in the long term.

Techniques to build confidence are useful for everyone, not only people with bipolar disorder. It's just that it is so easy to lose confidence when you swing between mania and depression with bipolar disorder, and as I've said before, the likelihood is you have embarrassed yourself more than once and you have to find a way back. Confidence techniques will help to achieve this.

Keep a positive image to fight off the negative side of bipolar disorder. Remember: *I am very beautiful. I am very powerful. And everybody loves me.*

CHAPTER SIX

The Recovery Process

This chapter looks at some of the drugs available for managing bipolar disorder. People with bipolar disorder usually try mood stabilizers first and continue treatment for many years, if not a lifetime. Lithium is a very effective mood stabilizer. In the United States, in the 1970s, it was the first mood stabilizer approved by the Food and Drug Administration (FDA) for treating both manic and depressive episodes.

Anticonvulsant medications also are used as mood stabilizers. They were originally developed to treat seizures, but they were found to help control moods as well. One anticonvulsant commonly used as a mood stabilizer is valproic acid (VPA), also called divalproex sodium, (brand names: Depakote, Depakene, Epilim, Stavzor). For some people, VPA may work better than lithium. Other anticonvulsants include carbamazepine (brand names: Tegretol, Epitol l, Equator, Carbatrol); lamotrigine (brand name: Lamictal); and oxcarbazepine (brand name: Trileptal).

Many times atypical antipsychotics are used in combination with a mood stabilizer. Here are a few that I have had experience with:

- **Olanzapine** (brand name: Zyprexa) helps people with severe or psychotic depression, which often is accompanied by a break from reality, hallucinations, or delusions.
- **Aripiprazole** (brand name: Abilify) can be taken as a pill or as a shot.
- **Risperidone** (brand name: Risperdal).

- **Ziprasidone** (brand name: Geodon).
- **Clozapine** (brand name: Clorazil, Fazaclo) is often used to treat people not responding to lithium or anticonvulsants.

In addition to the medications listed above, antidepressants are sometimes used to treat symptoms of depression in bipolar disorder. Commonly prescribed antidepressants include fluoxetine (brand names: Prozac, Rapiflux, Sarafem, Selfemra); paroxetine (brand names: Paxil, Pexeva); and sertraline (brand name: Zoloft).

Note: people with bipolar disorder should not take an antidepressant on its own. Doing so can cause someone with bipolar to rapidly swing from depression to mania, which can be dangerous. To prevent this problem, doctors give patients a mood stabilizer or an antipsychotic along with an antidepressant. In fact, the use of antidepressants to help manage bipolar disorder has yielded mixed results in research studies. In the United States, a NIMH-funded study found that antidepressants were no more effective than a placebo in helping treat depression in people with bipolar disorder, even when the patients were taking mood stabilizers in addition to the antidepressant.

You will experience different side effects when taking medication for bipolar disorder: everyone responds differently to medication. Drugs have improved over the last ten years, but if you do experience side effects, it is important to tell your doctor, so that he or she can change the dose or prescribe a different medication. Here are some of the most common side effects with popular bipolar medications:

Lithium

People with bipolar disorder who are being treated with lithium should visit the doctor regularly to check the levels of lithium in the blood and make sure the kidneys and the thyroid are working normally. Lithium can have serious side effects, including:

- Loss of coordination
- Excessive thirst
- Frequent urination
- Blackouts
- Slurred speech
- Fast, slow, irregular, or pounding heartbeat
- Hallucinations
- Changes in vision
- Itching
- Swelling of face

Valproic acid/divalproex sodium

Valproic acid may cause damage to the liver or pancreas, so people taking it should see their doctor regularly. Among the side effects are:

- Changes in weight
- Nausea
- Stomach pain
- Vomiting
- Anorexia
- Loss of appetite

The negative side effects are troublesome, and you will have to find ways of working with them. Bear in mind, though, not everyone gets all the side effects listed. There is no cure for bipolar disorder, but treatment works for many people.

It works best when it is continuous, rather than on and off; however, mood changes can happen even when there are no breaks in medication. Patients should be open with their doctors about their medication. Talking about treatment and how it is working with the health professionals can help it become more effective.

NOTE: never stop taking a medication without asking the doctor for guidance.

I have been taking antipsychotic drugs for the past eight years, and I can honestly say that I hate it. Why do I feel so strongly about this? Every morning and every evening, I have to pop pills. This may not seem to be a problem for anyone on the outside, but having to be a servant to the pills affects my mental state. I want to be free of all medication and be dependent on nothing other than myself. That is, of course, a dream. Still, I think it would be good if they could come up with a pill you take once a year, or even once a month, as you now can with osteoporosis medication—taking pills every day is wearing.

Each change of antipsychotic drug can bring different side effects. I have been on three different drugs, and all of them have caused problems at some stage of taking them.

Among the side effects I have experienced on antipsychotic drugs are:

Trembling hands

This has caused me problems on numerous occasions. The most difficult time is when I have to go to a business meeting and I have trouble lifting the cup of coffee. Another embarrassing time is having to go to the toilet and not being able to do up your trousers because your hands are trembling so much. Once I went out on a date with a young man and he offered me a drink. When it came to trying to pick up the glass of wine it was impossible. I had to ask him to do it for me. As you can imagine I did not get to see him again.

Dry mouth

My mouth gets so dry, I can drink gallons of water. Nothing makes a difference, and I've often looked like a crazed horse with my tongue hanging out. Once again this can be difficult when you are working. After drinking so much liquid, you can find yourself in a position where you constantly want to pee, which is not great for work.

Water is the best drink to quench your thirst, as it has no sodium and no sugar. If this doesn't work, I would suggest drinking peppermint tea, sports drinks, or lemon water.

Anxiety

I can become anxious and show a lack of patience when working with my colleagues, and this can be challenging. My anxiety will show itself in negative body language or tone of voice. I have to rely on my breathing techniques to relax me—breathe in through the nose and out through the mouth, remembering to do this to the count of three.

Reduced libido

I have noticed reduced libido. I am not in a relationship right now, so it is not so important; however, feeling unsexy does nothing for one's mental state.

Weight gain

Weight gain has to be one of the worse side effects for me. I have put on so much weight from taking different drugs, it is hard to remember being thin. As I said before, going from a UK size 10 to a size 18 has definitely sapped my confidence. I have taken myself off to Weight Watchers and Slimming World, to no avail. You could argue the case that over the years I would have put this weight on anyway, but I'm not sure that this is correct. My other bipolar friends also carry too much weight around the stomach area, and this I believe is down to the medication. On a positive note, I spend time walking and going to the gym to lose weight, and most recently I have taken up Zumba classes.

Spasms

This can be a difficult one at work. I remember once being in a business meeting and the person doing the presentation was just finishing when there was an almighty bang—I had had a spasm in my leg muscle and violently kicked the bottom of the table. The speaker ended his presentation rather abruptly!

My worst experience with antipsychotic drugs has been when I have been prescribed a dosage to control my mania that is too high for my tolerance level, which has happened on several occasions. You do have to be very careful how much you are prescribed. Antipsychotic drugs are used to prevent your mood from escalating too high. If you take too much, you can find yourself extremely anxious and zombie like.

One time, I had been prescribed too high a dosage of Ariprazole, and I had to pick up my son from school, a ten-minute drive from my house. I found myself in a very dangerous situation because I had become so anxious that I began to imagine that my feet were glued together and I couldn't reach the brake pedal. As I was coming down the hill towards his school, tears were running down my face. What was I going to do? I couldn't move my feet. Thankfully, the noise of an approaching police car with its siren on full blast broke through my fixation about my feet, got them moving normally again, and I was able to continue driving and pick up my son.

This was a really frightening experience and one that I would not like to repeat. The anxiety lasted for over a week and I could not drive for that period of time. After speaking to my doctor about my experience, I was able to reduce my tablets by 5 mgs, and, thankfully, that made all the difference.

As I mentioned before, I've tried three types of antipsychotic drugs: Risperidel, Seroquel XL, and Ariprazole. Risperidel made me feel like a zombie, no matter how little I took of it. Seroquel XL made me fat.

Ariprazole has been the best to date, although it does leave me with the shakes.

Taking antipsychotic medication is not all negative. As much as I do not want to have to take the tablets, I can rationalize and understand the benefits. When I was a young girl I suffered from mood swings and I have managed to live without antipsychotic medication until I was 42 years old and got diagnosed as bipolar.

I remember going out one evening with my friend Barbara, and we had decided to go to a jazz bar in London. The bar was really busy and the musicians were fantastic. As the night went on, I became high and wanted to get myself noticed. Without further ado, I stood up and took off my top, and ended up standing there in just my bra. My friend was used to my behaviour and tried to calm me down. Even though she found it funny, she did not want us to get thrown out of the bar. Too late. Seconds later, I had also taken off my bra and some heavy bouncers were headed towards us and we were thrown out!

This may sound amusing, but this sort of behaviour happened all the time when I was not on antipsychotic drugs. I never saw myself as a danger, although looking back I did do some crazy things that could have got me into trouble.

I can only reiterate how important it is to be patient with the trial and error required to get the type and dosage of medications right for you. As I stressed earlier, a good psychiatrist who listens to your feedback will help enormously, as will a good relationship with your care coordinator. It's important to have someone with whom you feel on the same wavelength, as this person sees you regularly and can offer feedback about drug reactions.

Tips to Increase Mental Health
and Physical Health

I have always found it a struggle to switch off and mentally relax. Over the years I have had to look for internal and external ways of looking after my mental health. Here are some of the ways I look after my mental and physical well-being:

Art

As a young girl I liked the feel of the paintbrush and doing art. This love affair came to an abrupt halt in secondary school, though, when I received a heartbreaking "Unclassified" grade in my Art O-level (one of the General Certificate of Education examinations, or GCEs, I took in order to graduate from my UK high school). That "unclassified" grade meant my work was so bad the board examiners did not grade it! As you can imagine, this had a profoundly negative effect on my desire and confidence to do art, and so I did not pick up a paintbrush again until I was 42 years old.

I share this sad story so that you can understand how much this kind of negative judgement of your creativity can affect your mental well-being. I now use art therapeutically to stay mentally well, and it has paid off: during the past eight years, I have created more than 50 oil paintings and had three art exhibitions, where I have sold my work. I paint in oils and love using colour. I paint on a regular basis now, which keeps me fresh and mentally agile. Painting is also an activity that can be done with others, so it becomes a social activity that can bring great joy to life.

Pottery

This is a great way to relax, both mentally and physically. The feel of the clay and moulding brings great mental benefits and is also quite grounding.

Going to the movies

Fantasy, reality, drama, thrillers, and other kinds of movies are really helpful in shifting your mood. Films are a great escape from the travails of this world, and over the years, I've found that watching movies has helped me improve my mental well-being.

Books

Reading is a wonderful activity; moreover, it costs nothing to read when you use your local library. Reading a variety of literature is good for the mind and stimulates the brain. My experience as someone with bipolar is that it is really difficult to read when you are either in mania or depression—concentrating is near impossible. In fact, when you find yourself attracted to reading again, that is a sign that you have come out of either mania or depression and are heading toward a more normal state.

Walking

What better way to stay well than taking a walk in the countryside? But if you live in a city, it can be just as beautiful. Again, going for a walk costs nothing, and it is something you can do with friends and family or simply on your own. I have found walking a godsend. Not only are you outside in the fresh air but it is widely acknowledged that sunlight is highly beneficial in the treatment of bipolar disorder, as sunlight on skin is essential to boosting the vitamin D levels in your body, important in maintaining the health of mind and body.

There have always been times in my life when my anxiety or depression has been at an all-time low and walking would be the only thing that would lift my mood. I have found even when I am manic that walking somehow calms me down and I am in a better place after a half-hour walk or longer.

In the UK, where sunlight is at a premium and generally weak, an hour a day of full-skin exposure to direct sunlight in the middle of the day, when the key UV rays are at their peak, is seen as helpful to mental outlook, particularly for patients who suffer from seasonal affective disorder (SAD) depression during the dark days of winter. People with bipolar should check their medications for interactions with sunlight; some may cause light sensitivity.

In places where the sun is strong, you should be sure to protect your head and neck with a hat, put on UV-blocking sunglasses to protect the eyes, and wear clothing that can be rolled down to protect your skin. Don't use sunblock whilst taking a therapeutic 10-15-minute daily sunbath—sunscreen blocks out the UV rays that are essential to manufacturing vitamin D in the skin. If the sun is strong and you are outdoors, take a sunbath and then add the sunblock or cover the skin with clothing for the rest of the day. In hot climates, you will need to adjust these recommendations for exposure; don't overdo it. For example, in desert climates such as the American Southwest, just 10-15 minutes of full-body exposure to sunlight yields the 10,000 I.U. of vitamin D essential to health.

> **NOTE**: Supplementing with vitamin D capsules is a different matter from getting vitamin D naturally through sunlight and foods like salmon, which contain small amounts. Vitamin D deficiency is a chronic problem in the UK and US, and it's a good idea to visit a doctor who will order a test. If you're too low, your doctor will suggest supplements as well as sunbaths to get your levels up for health. You can't overdose on natural sunlight, but you can on supplements. Be sure to work with a doctor if you are deficient.

Aerobic Activity

Aerobic workouts three times a week are highly recommended for anyone suffering from bipolar disorder, as aerobic activity helps stimulate endorphins, the natural mood enhancers in the brain. I have found that Zumba classes work for me. Not only do I have an aerobic work-out but also the music is extremely uplifting and stimulating and I meet new friends there.

Swimming

I have been doing fitness swims for the past 20 years, on and off, but it is only in the last five years that I have made swimming part of my exercise schedule. I now try to swim two to three times a week for half an hour at a time. I find this really helps my mental and physical well-being. It also makes me feel more confident as I stretch my muscles and feel empowered. Swimming is something you can do with the whole family, so you can include other people in keeping fit and well. Swimming is also a great way to help ideas flow when you need to be creative. It has many benefits, and I would strongly recommend it.

Healthy Diet

When do I really feel my best? I feel my best when I am eating a healthy diet of fresh fruit, fresh vegetables, oily fish, pulses, nuts and protein. Eating a sensible diet helps to keep me mentally and physically well. If I neglect myself and eat fast foods, the high levels of low-grade fats and simple sugars play havoc on my high blood sugar levels and that adds to my mental instability. I find another way of staying healthy is to enjoy cooking with friends and family. Cooking is a creative pastime and you get in touch with your senses; taste, touch, smell, this is good for your mental state once again.

Spending time with friends and family

Friends and family play a great part in keeping an individual both mentally and physically well. So when you are depressed, it is impor-tant to engage with friends and, as long as relations are healthy and supportive, your family. Conversation helps lift someone from the depths of depression. Even when you are in the manic phase of bipolar, it is still necessary to be around loved ones, as you move into a scary place of superhuman belief in yourself and need people around you who can keep you grounded. By having a strong network, you are more likely to make arrangements to go out and mix in the community, which is a good thing no matter where you are on the pole.

Other activities I came across when researching alternative activities for treating bipolar disorder range from horseback riding (equine therapy) to drumming groups. The common thread in these activities was rhythm and how it relates to dealing with the "rapid cycling" of bipolar patients.

Is Alternative Medicine an Option?

You should *always* speak to your doctor before trying any new form of medication, whether prescribed or complementary. To forego taking your prescribed medication and change to alternative medicine alone can be very dangerous: some herbs are contraindicated if you are taking antidepressants because of negative side effects.

Studies in the US and Canada have shown that a majority of the population are not getting anywhere near the recommended daily allowance (RDA) of vitamins C, E, A, D, and B-complex and the minerals zinc, magnesium, iron, copper, and calcium in the diet to support physical and mental health.

Holistic health practitioners, such as homeopaths, herbalists, naturopathic doctors, and Traditional Chinese Medicine (TCM), commonly recommend that people with bipolar manage the disease by improving their diet and taking nutritional supplements. There is documented evidence that these measures lead to improvements in functioning for those with bipolar disorder.

The following are some of the most recommended supplements for bipolar:

L-Tryptophan

This amino acid is needed to help produce serotonin in the brain, the neurotransmitter that helps to keep you calm. Eating foods rich in Tryptophan is much better than taking a supplement. Foods rich in Tryptophan are: turkey, complex carbohydrates such as whole grains, beans and pulses, nuts and dairy.

Omega-3 Fatty Acids

Omega-3 fatty acids are essential in maintaining good mental health. Due to the poor diets that we keep today many of us live on processed food, which does not contain enough omega-3 fatty acids. These can be found in wild salmon, sardines, mackerel, herring, eggs, dairy, meat and dark green leaf vegetables. To improve mental health you can take a supplement of a fish oil capsule daily.

B-complex vitamins

When trying to maintain a healthy balanced diet and you are not getting enough vitamins through the natural process, it is worth considering taking supplements of B-complex vitamins including B1 (thiamine), B2 (riboflavin), B6 (pyridoxine), B7 (biotin), B12 (cobalamin), and folic acid.

Research has shown that low folate levels could be connected to depression. Taking folic acid could be a good thing to consider if medical drugs like antidepressants send you into mania. B-complex vitamins are found in leafy greens like spinach and kale; beans; nuts; pastured meat, dairy, and eggs; and in the yeast extract spread Marmite.

Vitamin C

The Yale New Haven Health Complementary Medicine website

recommends: "...until more is known, people with Bipolar Illness should avoid supplements containing vanadium and consider supplementing with vitamin C."

Vitamin C is a strong antioxidant, which helps cleaning up free radicals that are released in the body through normal metabolism. It also supports repairing organs such as the adrenal glands, which manage the stress response. Vitamin C is now being examined for possible beneficial effects in people with bipolar, as it helps to clear the trace mineral vanadium from the body, which is sometimes abnormally high in people with bipolar. Taking vitamin C can help reduce their stress.

Good sources of vitamin C are colourful fruits and vegetables, such as peppers, broccoli, tomatoes, Brussels sprouts, sweet potatoes, oranges, and kiwi fruit. I have personally found eating more fresh fruit and vegetables very beneficial in dealing with my bipolar.

Vitamin E

It is suggested by some that people with bipolar disorder should consume more vitamin E if they are taking Depakote or another anticonvulsant, as these drugs deplete vitamin E. If your blood pressure rises simply reduce the amount of vitamin E you are taking (this vitamin is known for increasing blood pressure).

Vitamin E can be found in the following foods: plant oils, such as soya, corn, and olive oil, nuts such as almonds, seeds, and wheat germ.

Vitamins A and D

Both of these vitamins are fat-soluble, i.e. they can be stored in the body's fat cells for later use. If you do not get enough vitamin A or D you can take it via supplements, including fish oil and cod liver oil; however, avoid taking too much.

Good sources of vitamin A include cheese, eggs, mackerel and other oily fish, milk, and yoghurt. Liver is a particularly rich source of vitamin A.

A lack in Vitamin D can lead to depression, fatigue and sleep disorders; thus this vitamin is especially important for people with bipolar. A good source is sunlight (in moderate dosages). Foods rich in vitamin D are milk, cereals, salmon, eggs and orange juice.

Magnesium

Magnesium is essential to ensure the body maintains a healthy function: the mineral maintains normal nerve and muscle function, and helps keeping the heart rhythm steady and the bones healthy. It also regulates blood sugar levels and promotes normal blood pressure.

Taking magnesium will help people with bipolar disorder through alleviating their nerves. The best food sources for magnesium are dark green leafy vegetables and whole grains.

Zinc

Adequate levels of zinc are important for a well-functioning immune system, while low levels may even contribute to depression. Zinc is available in chewable supplements as well as in food. Good food sources are shellfish (in particular oysters), red meat and poultry; beans, nuts, whole grains, and dairy products.

Herbs and Supplements

Chamomile and Valerian Root

Discuss with your doctor first to see whether herbs will work for you. Chamomile and Valerian Root are extremely calming and particularly useful for depression as well as anxiety and sleeplessness. It is not advisable to take Valerian Root alongside pharmaceutical medication. St. John's wort though is NOT recommended for bipolar disorder, because antidepressants of any type, herbal or pharmaceutical, can so rapidly plunge people with bipolar into depression or mania.

Taurine

Taurine is an amino acid. Amino acids are found in high-quality proteins and literally feed your brain by promoting proper neurotransmitter function that allows the brain to communicate with the body through the nervous system. Taurine is a relaxing amino acid that calms you down when you are stressed. Food sources include: fish, meat and sea algae.

GABA

This is a relaxing amino acid that counters adrenaline and supports restful sleep and dreaming. It also helps with stress and burnout.

L-Glutamine

This amino acid is primarily responsible for keeping blood sugar in the brain stable, as the brain burns glutamine when it runs out of glucose in a hypoglycemic state. It promotes calm alertness. If you eat a lot of sweets, drink caffeine, skip meals, and otherwise have poor dietary habits, this may be a useful supplement.

Melatonin

This hormone is produced in the pineal gland and controls the sleep-wake cycle. Melatonin is made from serotonin, which is one of the major neurotransmitters in the brain that is in charge of mood. You often find that people with depression will have low serotonin and melatonin levels which will lead to sleeplessness and an interrupted sleep-wake rhythm. Foods that include melatonin are: oats, sweet corn, rice, ginger and barley, tomatoes, bananas, radishes, fruits and vegetables, almonds and seeds. Melatonin supplements are only effective if they are taken before it gets dark.

5HTP

5HTP is the converted form of the amino acid tryptophan and is a precursor to serotonin, the feel-good neurotransmitter that is so often deficient in people with depression and bipolar. 5HTP has been used very successfully in treating depression and should strongly be considered as a frontline natural treatment for depression and bipolar. It is also an excellent sleep aid, because of its role in boosting serotonin and melatonin.

Ashwagandha

Sometimes called Indian ginseng this particular herb assists the body where needed. It can calm you down and help you sleep when taken at night or help you focus your awareness when taken during the day, without making you drowsy. However, make sure you talk to your doctor before taking Ashwagandha as it may react in combination with other medication. Note: This herb is not advisable for breastfeeding or pregnant women.

SAM-E (S-adenosylmethionine)

This amino acid positively affects neurotransmitters in the brain. A 2010 study cited on the healing with whole foods website myhealingkitchen.com found that "36 percent of patients taking a combination of SAM-e and an antidepressant showed improvement, compared to just 18 percent of those taking the antidepressant and placebo. And about 26 percent of patients in the SAM-e group experienced a complete remission of symptoms, compared to just 12 percent in the placebo group. If you are taking other medications or have bipolar disorder, be sure to check with your doctor before taking SAM-e."

Theanine

This supplement is made from green tea. It is very effective in promoting a calm yet aware feeling and also counters caffeine and stimulants, including high cortisol, the body's stress hormone.

Homeopathy

Homeopathy is a system of medicine that works through the law of similars: treating the individual with highly diluted substances in tiny sugar pill form that antidote a condition in the body, with the aim of triggering the body's natural system of healing. Homeopaths treat patients on the basis of their constitutions, not as a one-size-fits-all protocol for certain symptoms, and match the most appropriate medicine to each patient.

Patients initially take the remedy for a period of two to five weeks (a single dose can work immediately, if it is the correct one for that patient's unique constitution). If symptoms persist, your homeopath will suggest a new remedy. According to naturopath and homeopath Dr. Reichenberg-Ullman, ND, who with her husband Richard Ullman, ND, is a world-renowned authority on homeopathy, treatment must be continued for a minimum of one to two years in order to rebalance the patient's entire constitution.

There are no side effects: either the remedy works or it doesn't. Substances containing menthol, camphor, coffee, and eucalyptus may interfere with homeopathic remedies and should usually not be taken at the same time as the remedy. Prescription medications, however, do not usually interfere with the effectiveness of the remedy. Some doctors will also use antibiotics, topical steroids, and other cortisone products in combination with the remedies, if needed. Homeopathy can be a reassuring mind-body-spirit approach to treating bipolar disorder and should be investigated.

Bodywork

Craniosacral Therapy

This is a subtle form of healing that focuses on the intrinsic rhythms and fluid movements in the craniosacral system. You usually lie down fully clothed on a treatment couch and the therapist will make contact by placing their hands lightly on your body and tuning in to the body's subtle expressions. The first thing you will probably notice is a deep sense of relaxation, which will generally last throughout the session and often extends into everyday life.

Levels of trauma can be shifted in this way and the body can be activated into a deeper slower pace of being. Working alongside other practitioners like doctors and hospital personnel the therapist can help clients with bipolar disorder or depression by reconnecting them to their inner self in a safe way. Note: This therapy would not be recommended for a client who is going through a manic phase or a very depressed phase of bipolar.

Massage

Having a massage is one of the best things you can do for body, emotions and mind. A massage can relieve stress by lowering cortisol levels in the body and also improve circulation and thus the supply of oxygen and nutrients to organs and tissue.

In addition, pressure points touched during the massage release endorphins, which leaves you feeling good and brings a more positive outlook on life. A massage is strongly recommended if you suffer from the down side of bipolar.

Aromatherapy Massage

At the heart of aromatherapy lies the work with essential oils that are used therapeutically to help alleviate a variety of symptoms and ailments. It is these oils that stimulate the hypothalamus in the brain, which regulates our hormonal system; feel-good hormones are released that help relax the person.

This type of massage is highly recommended for people suffering from bipolar. Here are some essential oils that are often used for the treatment of bipolar disorder:

Lavender

Lavender oil can have a calming effect on people who are agitated and irritable. A gentle massage with this oil can promote a deep relaxing sleep, which again supports a more balanced nervous system.

Jasmine

Anxiety can be relieved by the delicate smell of jasmine flowers. This oil creates an uplifting atmosphere and promotes a feeling of happiness and confidence.

Rosemary

Rosemary has an antioxidant effect and protects the body from the inflammatory action of free radicals, which are triggered by poor nutrition and stress as well as by injuries and disease. Blood circulation can be strengthened by taking a bath with a few drops of rosemary oil in the water; this can also help to calm and soothe frayed nerves.

Frankincense

This essential oil is often used in meditation and end-of-life transitions, and generally very helpful for quietening the mind. Also a very potent anti-cancer oil, frankincense has very useful properties.

Grapefruit

Grapefruit (and other citrus oils, such as orange) have a fresh, slightly stimulating smell and lead to feelings of light euphoria. Because of this, citrus oils can be used to hold depression at bay while helping to promote positive feelings.

The above information is designed to offer some general suggestions on natural treatments that many bipolar patients have found helpful. You will find more good information on such treatments for bipolar in

Stephanie Marohn's very helpful and well-researched book *The Natural Medicine Guide to Bipolar Disorder* (Hampton Roads Publishing, 2003).

On my own healing journey, I must admit I have so far not had a lot of success using herbs and supplements. In the past, my main mistake has been in not discussing my intentions with my doctor first. I did what is not advisable: I combined herbal supplements with prescribed medications and did not get good results. If you are bipolar, it is very important that you don't take natural herbal antidepressants AND prescribed antidepressants at the same time, which is what I was doing. Complementary medicine is just that: it is supposed to complement mainstream medicine, so it's essential to work with holistic doctors conversant with both pharmaceutical and natural medicines who are aware of contraindications for certain remedies.

I first tried using St John's wort (*hypericum perforatum*), a common herbal antidepressant that has been used successfully in Europe for many years to treat mild to moderate depression. Unfortunately, because of the nature of my bipolar disorder, I found myself shooting down into the depths of depression with this herb and it didn't work for me. Next, I stopped taking my lithium and replaced it with zinc and magnesium supplements. In this case, I found myself shooting up into mania.

It's important to reiterate that I took this course of action on my own and did not speak to my doctor, so it's true to say that I did not give alternative medicine a chance to work for me. I believe that a mixture of therapies *can* work, as long as you work closely with both medical and complementary health professionals.

A Walk in the Woods

CHAPTER SEVEN

Disabling Aspects
of Bipolar Disorder –
Case Studies

When I told other people with bipolar that I was writing this book, they were only too happy to share their stories with me and let me know their greatest concerns in managing their illness. Most people with bipolar whom I spoke to said that losing their job was their biggest fear. Another area of concern that they expressed was keeping good relationships with their wife/husband/siblings and friends.

Here is Shaun's story:

I have been a single man all my life. I had been diagnosed with bipolar when I was 18 years old, so I was used to the highs and lows. My main trait was to go into mania.

I have only ever experienced one depression, which was terrible. I was working as a consultant for an engineering company and I had experienced a lot of stress in my life. The girl I was in love with was no longer in love with me, and I was heartbroken. I had also invested in a new car that had broken down after a few days, and the stress had started to build up.

Whilst I was at work, I started to see everyone in combat gear. I thought I was at war with the enemy, and that happened to be the staff. I started to throw office objects across the room, believing they were grenades. At this point, I was thrown to the ground by my boss and put into the manager's office. The police were called, along with a psychiatric doctor, and I was "sectioned" and admitted to hospital.

Up until that point, my employers did not know about my condition, and that was how I would have kept it. I was "sectioned" and spent the next two months in hospital. I was very lucky that I kept my job, though now people know about my illness I no longer want to be there. Everyone treats me differently.

Shaun found this a very disabling experience. He had always been private about his mental illness, and now he had to be open about it. Shaun has found that he is discriminated against because of his illness. He explained to me that most people have no idea about mental illness. The moment the word is mentioned, you are labelled as "crazy," or worse, "mad."

When I interviewed Mary, I found she also experienced disabling aspects with the illness:

I was diagnosed with bipolar disorder when I was 35 years old. Although this is late to be diagnosed, I was prone to suffering from depression. It was only when I had a full-blown manic episode [that] bipolar was diagnosed.

When I was diagnosed I had been married for several years and had two great boys, who are now aged 21 and 24. The boys had been used to seeing me depressed and were very good at trying to lift Mummy's mood. It was very distressing for them to see me manic. During this manic episode, I was hospitalized for two months and this started my ongoing journey with bipolar.

I am now 55 and have been in a psychiatric hospital five times. Each time since has been for depression. When I suffer from depression, I want to commit suicide, so have to be hospitalized for my own good.

I have found the illness very disabling, and it has affected my family life. My boys are my life, though they worry about me a great deal. Both boys still live at home, and I do wonder if I did not have this illness would they have flown the nest.

I have always been a full-time mum. Once again, due to the illness, I would have been unable to hold down a job. I could not work if I had wanted to. My husband has recently spoken of divorce, as he can't cope any longer with the mood swings. I feel extremely let down by him, though I understand, as I find it hard to live with the mood swings myself.

Mary is still suffering from depression and finds it hard to live with the illness.

Louise, on the other hand, has a very different story to tell:

I have run my own recruitment company for the past 20 years. I love running my own company. My company is highly successful, though financially it has been incredibly challenging.

I've always been a very independent person. I like to be self-motivated and to rely on my own resources. I'm single out of choice. I've found when I have had a boyfriend they have not understood my manic moments.

I was diagnosed with bipolar when I was 25, and I am 49 now. During my time with the illness, I have experienced three episodes of mania that have led me to be hospitalized.

I have destroyed my financial empire with each episode of mania. During the first episode of mania, I found myself gambling large sums of money at a casino. This, I find, has become my key indicator informing me of when I am going into a manic episode.

I have been unable to stop myself gambling during these manic times, and it is this that has brought my company down financially.

I have found the illness very disabling at times. The only positive I can find about the illness is I always come back with new ideas after a manic moment. I still would sell my illness to anyone who would buy it. I hate having bipolar.

Roger tells his story:

I've worked in print all my life, and everyone knows I'm a big personality. I've always suffered from mood swings: I was either very high or very low. Everyone used to say: "Roger, he is never on the same level as the rest of us. He is always swinging high or low."

I was 43 when they diagnosed me as bipolar. I had been out at the pub with my friends and had drunk quite a lot. I had become rather manic. During the evening with my friends, they encouraged me to do something daring. I readily obliged, went into the toilets, and came out stark naked! "What's the problem?" I thought, though they were absolutely gobsmacked. My descent into mania had begun.

I have a very loving wife, who has put up with me for over 20 years. Recently, I asked her if she could change anything about me what it would be. To my surprise, she said she would have me no other way. For me, it is hard to live with the illness, but for my wife, she takes it in her stride.

I suffer from both depression and mania and swing regularly along the axis. I have had a rough time with side effects and have put on over five stone [70 pounds] due to medication. I've tried an assortment of diets and drugs, and nothing seems to work.

I was happier before I was diagnosed with the illness. I hate having to take drugs. I preferred my body shape before being diagnosed. Having this illness makes me angry.

Rita tells her story:

> I was raised in a large family and love having friends and family around.
>
> I had been friends with Carol since school, and she knew me better than I knew myself. Carol had always appreciated my funny quirky behaviour and encouraged me to do mad things.
>
> I was diagnosed with bipolar, when I had my first manic episode that led me into a psychiatric ward. I believed I was Martin Luther King and went around recruiting people from the street to fight the good cause.
>
> Carol found these episodes funny and would encourage me to be as crazy as possible. Life with Carol was fine whilst I experienced mania.
>
> When I started to get depressed, Carol was sad to lose her whacky friend, and didn't understand depression. When I needed her most, she was not there to help. I found that the depression had a detrimental effect on my relationship with my best friend.
>
> I am no longer friends with Carol, though the rest of my family and friends have been extremely supportive and have been able to understand my condition and be there for me.

From these stories of people living with bipolar, I think you can see how destructive the illness can be. It is so important for loved ones and friends to try to understand bipolar. It would help, I think, if there were more support groups for friends and family of those with bipolar. There are lots of places for friends and family of alcoholics to get help, including Al-Anon; the loved ones of those with bipolar need the same support.

How to Handle the Constant
Roller Coaster of Mood Swings

I have been spinning out of orbit for the past eight years. One minute, I will be in mania, then down into the depths of depression. There is no easy way to handle the roller coaster.

The first thing you have to do is accept the diagnosis and confront it head on. Once you know the symptoms you can try to treat the cause. As you move through the different cycles of the illness, then medication comes into play. Normally, an increase in your mood stabilizer and antipsychotic is necessary.

If you are facing depression, an antidepressant is a possibility but, as discussed earlier, most health professionals do not want to prescribe an antidepressant in case it leads to mania. It's essential to be careful and work closely with health professionals.

What helps me manage my mood swings is keeping a diary, so that I can see if a pattern emerges. I have to say it has. I can almost guarantee every May/June, I will head towards a manic or depressive episode. This is helpful for health professionals, family, and friends to know, as they can then all be on red alert. In my cycle, I find it much harder to detect a depressive mood—they seem to come out of the blue.

I struggle with the depressive aspect of the illness, as it stops me dead in my tracks. I am used to being a high flyer with an independent outlook on life. Finding myself in the depths of despair, unable to get out of bed, unable to cook, unable to function without the help of my family and friends is quite distressing.

During bad times, my care coordinator comes to see me once a week, which really helps me. Together, we can keep on top of the mood swings and book an emergency appointment with my psychiatrist, if need be. When I start to improve, my care coordinator will then reduce her visits to once a month. My care coordinator is particularly helpful in helping me manage my mood swings. Often you don't spot your key indicators, because you are the one living with the illness. A good care coordinator will spot the changes. It could be subtle changes in vocal tone, ability to make eye contact, or the house being either dirty or obsessively clean.

My care coordinator tries her best to spot my key indicators, although this has not always been the case as I am very good at covering my tracks. I remember one particular mood swing where I became psychotic. It all happened quite quickly.

I was working in Paris for a top construction company and living in Kent, so I had to travel by rail to France from Ashford International Railway Station frequently. I was used to making this journey, as I had worked for the company for the past six years. I had always succeeded in doing a great job every time I went there. I worked as a presentation coach for the senior management team, which was high stress. At the time, I was also experiencing stress at home, as my eldest daughter was suffering from depression.

No one at my client's company in Paris knew that I suffered from bipolar disorder, but while I was working there on one occasion, I started to feel a mood swing developing into psychosis during a coffee break. I took myself off to the local coffee shop away from the office, and whilst I was there, I started to hear a voice in my head telling me that I was the goddess Athena. I then went to a *patisserie* and bought 20 heart chocolates and a red sash.

When I returned to work, I had become very hyper and anxious. I was still able to work—but on the flip chart paper I drew hearts and told my client that the heart represented passion. Everyone bought into this, and they loved the fact that I had bought them a chocolate heart—no one was aware that I thought I was the goddess Athena.

My mania started to build. Whilst working with the chairman of the company, I started to put Greek codes on his speech, which was very hard to explain away, although I tried my best. My client sensed something was wrong, though, and suggested I rest.

I left the building and found myself walking around Paris, trying to engage with passers-by. I nearly got myself in trouble with a couple of Frenchmen who were looking for some loving. Fortunately, as the goddess Athena, I felt these men were beneath me, and so I did not go with them.

As the afternoon wore on, my spending began to escalate, as I felt compelled to buy clothes to enact the role of Athena. I bought a long white dress, sandals, gold earrings, and a pack of playing cards to use as "dare cards." If I turned an even card I had to physically touch someone. This sounds difficult to do, but I didn't find it difficult at all. I would go up to people and shake their hand, or I would offer a kiss to the waiter, amongst other things.

I was staying in Paris overnight, as I had to continue working with the management team the next morning. Due to my manic mood, I could not sleep and went out to eat on my own. I was becoming more and more erratic and removed from reality.

During the evening meal, I met a gentleman called Jean Paul who guessed something was not quite right. He asked my name, and I said "Athena," of course.

We had a good night talking and discussing life's events. He asked me back to his hotel room for a drink. I thought he was of the right class so I went with him. This was very dangerous and I found myself in a very sticky situation. Jean Paul wanted to make love, but I only wanted "platonic love"—after all, I was the goddess Athena and I could not be touched by mere mortals.

I couldn't get Jean Paul to understand that I only wanted our encounter to be platonic. He was so worked up at this point that I felt the only way to resolve the situation was to make love to him to keep him happy. As the goddess Athena, I was not frightened by this because I felt that my special powers would protect me. I felt I was doing the only thing I could.

The next morning I went back to my hotel. I was completely wrecked, having had no sleep the night before. I got ready for work, putting on my white dress and red sash, gold earrings, and sandals—a completely inappropriate outfit for the job I was doing, as you can imagine.

When I entered the building, all eyes were on me, but I explained to my work colleagues that I had dressed this way to communicate a feeling of grandeur, just as they needed to do when they spoke in public. My clients then understood what I was trying to achieve and didn't worry about my dress.

I managed to get through the day without causing too much havoc. I'm sure, looking back, I caused a stir, but they just put it down to "Whacky Hodges."

The psychotic episode did not stop there. When I got on the cross-channel train, I started to do a rain dance, which lasted all the way from Paris to Ashford. The passengers looked on in amazement. I certainly know I must have looked crazy.

When I arrived at Ashford, I had to drive back to Farningham to pick up my children. On the way, I stopped at a garage and bought five potted plants, then went to various churches off the M20 and placed the plants outside the buildings, believing that I was offering a symbol of love to all the children who had died.

This detour added two hours to my journey, and I was late picking up the children from my sister Jill's house. When I arrived, she knew immediately that something was wrong and suggested I stay over. She knew I needed to see my mental health care team. I didn't want to admit it, but I knew she was right.

I decided to stay at Jill's house, and the following day we went for an emergency meeting with my psychiatrist, who confirmed I was in mania and recommended I go for a short stay in hospital. My sister Jill would hear nothing of it and offered me a place at her home for a further few days until the mania lifted. My doctor prescribed extra antipsychotic drugs, which made me calmer. I stayed at my sister's house for five days and loving members of my family nursed me back to health.

There is no doubt that mood swings and psychosis are potentially dangerous. You have to be aware and try to spot them as soon as you can. This is where a mood swing diary is useful.

How to Turn Negative Feedback
in the Workplace into Positive

My story about what happened in Paris raises a big question: Should you let your work colleagues know about your mental disorder? Those of us who have been brought up well learn that telling the truth is the best option. However, there is still a stigma against mental health issues in the workplace. Ignorance is the basis for most of the stigma, and the best way to overcome it is to confront it head on by speaking about the illness, how it affects you, and what people should expect to happen. Then ask your colleagues what they expect the problems will be and how they think it will affect your ability to work.

Even though I said earlier that I prefer not to disclose my bipolar status, there is something very positive about having the courage to speak up about it, so that you are not living a lie. Your openness helps colleagues understand the illness. One way you can do that is to sit down at a computer and research the illness together on the Internet. Yes, you will find alarming stories that may frighten your colleagues, but this is your opportunity to describe your own experience of the disease and offer a perspective on the disorder.

Remember: bipolar can make you highly creative. Let your colleagues know that when you go into hypomania you produce up to 75 percent more work. This is a great advantage for any company.

Mental illness only seems to be all negative; in fact, the opposite is true. When you really look closer at people with bipolar disorder, you find that they are highly sensitive and creative human beings. They have the ability to work at high speed and with a sense of confidence that is second to none.

So how do you respond to a colleague who says, "You're mad?" Well, artist Vincent Van Gogh—the one who cut off his ear—was "mad" and look at what he achieved in his life! People from all walks of life have had bipolar disorder. Look at Winston Churchill, who suffered terrible depression (what he called his "black dog"), yet accomplished so much as prime minister at a key time in British history. And then there are actors Richard Dreyfuss, Ruby Wax, and Stephen Fry . . . to name but a few well-known public figures who suffer from bipolar disorder. Being called "mad" is, admittedly, difficult to deal with. It can leave you feeling angry and aggressive and misunderstood. But if you choose to see the concept of "mad" as a compliment about your creativity, it helps you deal with other people's ignorance.

In short: keep people informed. Discuss openly any questions or problems they may have about your bipolar status. And help them understand mental health issues.

Fly High

CHAPTER EIGHT

Enabling Aspects of Bipolar Disorder

As a young girl I was always known as the one with loads of energy. I wanted to become a famous actress—that was my dream. Coming from a working-class background and wanting to go to drama college was not the norm. I had no idea drama colleges even existed, let alone how to choose one and apply. Back then, the Internet did not yet exist.

Thankfully, when I went out to work at the age of 17, I met a great variety of people. They helped me achieve my dream of being an actress by telling me about drama colleges and assisting me with filling in the college application forms.

I was very privileged because film directors Stephen Spielberg and Lord David Puttnam back then were young men who worked at Collett Dickenson and Pearce, the advertising agency I worked for, and I would meet them on a regular basis. They both recognized that I had an abundance of energy and an enthusiasm for drama, and they told me that they could not see me doing a secretarial job for long. Lord David Puttnam, in particular, helped me find a good drama school. It was quite unbelievable that this man, with all his talents, would have the time to help me, but I think he did so because I stood out from the crowd.

I worked as secretary to 15 creative executives at the agency. I was supposed to be the person with logical and administration skills, but on numerous occasions, I would forget to relay messages, serve coffee instead of tea, and generally make a "pig's ear" of being a secretary.

I was, however, really respected for having the right attitude, energy, passion, and creative ideas—a result, I believe now, of being in hypomania at that time.

I left the agency to go to the Webber Douglas Academy to study drama. One of my classmates at the academy was actor Ross Kemp, who later became famous for playing Grant Mitchell in the popular British television series *East Enders*. Ross and I took part in the same theatre productions, and we were both hungry to find an agent.

Agents would come to the academy searching for new talent. I was in hypomania for the whole three years I was at Webber Douglas Academy, always full of ideas, and would stand out in any production. It wasn't long before an agent noticed me and signed me up. When I asked him why he had chosen me, he said that he noticed my ability straight away and believed I was "all heart." Being signed with an agent offered my first opening into the world of professional acting.

There were times at The Academy that I didn't see eye to eye with the drama teacher. I would mess around in the classroom, playing the fool and being disruptive. As a punishment, she would ask me to go away and learn to recite several pieces of Shakespeare. This was no trouble for me—I had a whole repertoire of speeches I knew by heart, and learning lines was simple for me in my hypomanic state. Unfortunately, my classmates were not as lucky: if they got into trouble alongside me and were asked to recite lines or speeches, they would really struggle.

I loved being able to act and take my mind into another world—it was often in a different place anyway, due to my hypomania. But being an actress gave me permission to be someone else, and this gave me great confidence and a yearning to become a really famous actress.

Having an agent led to many opportunities in my acting career. One of the best was auditioning for the film *Castaway* with the late Oliver Reed. I remember on the day, I had got overexcited and I started to become hypomanic. I hopped trains on the way there and got totally lost. I got so confused about where I was supposed to be that, in the end, I had to get a cab to the studios, which cost a near fortune.

In my audition, I had to demonstrate being able to speak both slang and the Queen's English. Slang was no problem, as I had been brought up in Bermondsey in South London, where slang was spoken on a daily basis. But when it came to the Queen's English, I struggled. The director wanted me to say "*lit-tle*" in an educated voice, but because I was feeling so high and not able to focus on the job in hand, it came out as "*lit'l*"—Bermondsey girl that I was.

I was not offered the part, sad to say. It was devastating because until that point all my hypomanic moments had helped me get the jobs I applied for. My father was very happy about this, mind you, as I would have spent the majority of the film in the nude!

Shortly after that experience, I auditioned for a TV show with Larry Grayson called *Mr and Mrs*. Once again, the fact that I was getting the opportunity to act increased my creativity and confidence. I always remember Larry Grayson being very high himself, so we hit it off really well! Once again, Larry Grayson noticed my energy and passion. This time I was able to take direction well and listen to what was required of me.

The TV show involved three "couples," a celebrity panel, and the audience. There was a lot of audience participation. Each couple would be asked a selection of questions by Larry Grayson, and it was the audience's job to guess from the answers which couple was really married.

The man who played my partner on the show and I were not the real married couple, of course. Unfortunately, with the answers we gave, the audience guessed early on in the programme that we were not really married, which meant the end of my starring role.

So my hypomania can be instrumental in getting me job opportunities. My enthusiasm and abundance are noticed on a regular basis, and this in turn enables me to be confident, forthright, and self-believing.

As well as giving me the confidence to go for acting work, my hypomania allowed me to have increased work capacity. This enabled me to start and run my own business. This took a lot of courage and energy, both of which I had in copious amounts, which I put down to hypomania.

I wanted to start a presentation skills company, where I could use my acting skills to enable business people to present to an audience with impact. I interviewed people on the street as part of my market research, testing out the name Up Front for my company. To my amazement, the name went down a storm. My mind was swimming with ideas—Money Up Front, Delivery Up Front, and so on.

I had to cold-call hundreds of companies to get business, but I was like a runaway train: nothing could stop me. It took a lot of confidence to do this. I would use the *Financial Times FTSE 100* as a directory for finding the top 100 companies and research who was the training manager, then call them directly and ask for business.

I put the early success of Up Front down to my hypomania and the fact that I could do a hundred jobs at once. I was also in charge of the creative solution for Up Front. I would design training programmes that other people could eventually deliver. This took a lot of effort and commitment. I also made sure I designed training techniques that were fresh and hadn't been tried before, as I wanted to be unique. Bringing props into the workplace was one area that was unique to Up Front.

I know that without my hypomania it would not have been possible to build a company so quickly. I did every job in the company for a period of time, and that takes a certain kind of mentality. I have found bipolar disorder to be really enabling when it comes to running a business. It manages to fire me up and gives me creative powers and a confidence that I would not have without the disorder.

Tapping into Your Creative Resources

It has been argued that some people are creative and some are not. But I believe we are all creative; it's just that some people are more confident in using their creativity, and therefore they just *appear* to be more creative.

The key to tapping into your creative resources is to do one thing differently each day to keep you fresh. These things can be small or large. It can be as simple as changing the newspaper you read, driving a different route to work, or watching an action film instead of a romance. This keeps you fresh and the creative juices flowing.

Another way of boosting creativity is to mix with as many different types of people as possible. This will give you other perspectives on things. Changing your environment is a must. This helps you see the world from a different angle and helps you challenge the norm. During my most creative times, I have lived and worked in Spain; retreated to my caravan in Monkton, near Canterbury, Kent; and taken weekend breaks to places like Barcelona and Paris. This has really helped my creative process.

In fact, being bipolar is a licence for creativity. When I am hypomanic, I am at my most creative. I find myself painting into the early hours of the morning, writing, developing business ideas, and generally tapping into my creative resources. Over the past eight years, I have achieved great works of art, written a book, and begun a new business.

Hypomania is the place you go to before mania, and if you could bottle this place it would be worth a fortune. The only way I can describe hypomania is to relate it to a battery that needs recharging. As you recharge the battery, the energy gets stronger and stronger, until you are ready to burst, and then you arrive in mania.

As I mentioned earlier, I have found that there are times in my life that I am less creative than others. I find it very hard to create when I am having a depressive episode. I often find it impossible to operate at all. What I will say is that when I come out of the depression I am renewed and ready to tackle any new task. The lesson I take from this is that everything has a flip side. You just have to be patient, and creativity will knock on your door once again.

I also find it useful to take classes in subjects that interest me. For two years, I took a weekly three-hour oil painting class in Sevenoaks, Kent. This class gave my creativity a new lease of life, and I produced many oil paintings on canvas that I was very proud of. The other positive about participating in that class was meeting like-minded people who were all passionate about art. Collectively, they helped my creative process. I also found visiting art galleries and studying other artists' work really rewarding.

Another creative outlet I have found has been my weekly writing classes. These classes help would-be writers publish their work, both in magazines and books. Once again, being with people who share my passion for the subject has helped my writing process. Writing can be a very solitary existence.

I have found that having structure in my life and regular activities in my diary support my creativity. The repetition—whether it be taking regular art or writing classes at the same time each week—helps me keep my creative juices flowing. Creativity is a state of mind. You have to believe in yourself and trust your instincts. As I've said I believe everyone is creative; just not everyone knows how to tap into it.

EXERCISE TO TRY AT HOME: **Journaling**
A good way to tap into your creative resources is to keep a daily journal. You can write about anything—the more mundane, the better. You do not want to think too much about what you want to say, so the more stream of consciousness the better. You are trying to tap into your subconscious.

The key to this journaling exercise is that you don't read the pages for three months. You then review them and see what your desires are, what you feel angry about, what you want to change, and so on. It gives you insight into your subconscious and allows you to see things differently.

Confidence to Make Things Happen

Confidence is a big subject to cover when it comes to living and working with bipolar. The biggest problem I find when I am in a hypomanic state is that my confidence is inflated. This can be positive, as it gets me to do things I would not normally have the confidence to do, but it can also be negative, because sometimes an inflated ego can lead you into sticky situations.

I remember one such instance that doesn't sound that bad but did have consequences.

I was meeting with my client in his office to discuss training senior members of his board. The idea was that I would teach them techniques that would allow them to make a winning presentation, and this would enable them to outbid their competitors on a multi-million pound deal. The meeting was going really well, and I was becoming higher as time went on. I started to believe I was Margaret Thatcher, and everything in the office belonged to me.

My client was totally unaware of my thoughts, as even with mania developing, I could still conduct a professional meeting. At one point during the day, I had to complete some paperwork and picked up my client's solid gold pen to sign my name. I then put the pen in my bag—after all I was Margaret Thatcher... everything in the office was mine, including the pen.

When I arrived back in my office I had received a call from my client saying he had misplaced his solid gold pen, which his wife had bought him as a 25th wedding anniversary present. He was beside himself and asked if I remembered using the pen. Had I picked it up by mistake? Thankfully, by this time I no longer was convinced that I was Margaret Thatcher and was horrified to realize that I had picked up his prize pen.

I called my client and apologized profusely, which he accepted graciously. I said that I had picked up the pen inadvertently. I hired a bike courier and had the pen delivered to him as soon as possible. I am sure he was very pleased, as he wouldn't have wanted to explain the loss of the pen to his wife!

As you can see from this story, the high that led me to have an overwhelming amount of confidence and belief in my being Margaret Thatcher could have got me in serious trouble.

During the 22 years I ran my corporate training business, I held meetings with board chairmen, CEOs, and managing directors. Having confidence has really helped me build a successful business and enabled me to feel on a par with and able to deliver a service to these individuals.

I remember one meeting where the company wanted to hire me as a presentation coach. I was sitting with six managers and the chairman around a very long table. We were discussing their annual review meeting and how they wanted to present their material with my help. During the meeting I listened very carefully. The meeting required me to stand up and demonstrate certain voice and structural techniques, which I presented really well.

I was receiving all the positive signs of being successfully hired until I mentioned my price: £3,000 per day (my, what confidence I had in myself!). At this point, the managers were in shock and wanted to negotiate the price. I explained they had the best in the market, and with that I started to pack up and walk to the exit door.

It was my complete confidence in myself that got the entire management team to ask me to come back to the table for negotiations. At that point, I knew I had won the deal and they were prepared to pay the money.

Sometimes, however, my unshakeable belief in myself has prevented me from listening properly and I have messed up big time.

I remember when I was a young woman working at the advertising agency, before I was diagnosed with bipolar (I believe I've had this illness since I was 21 years old). I was asked by my boss to buy flowers for a commercial the agency was making which was to be set in Amsterdam. I asked what flowers they wanted and how many? My boss replied: "One hundred tulips, of course. Remember the song 'Tulips From Amsterdam'."

I took the money and got myself a taxi to a nearby florist and ordered 100 roses. Then I boldly came back to my boss. Mission accomplished, so I thought. He would understand roses were far grander than tulips and that I knew far more than he did!

I remember him standing there with mouth open, looking down at the flowers, saying: "Lynn, this is my shoot, not yours. We are shooting a commercial set in Amsterdam. We require tulips, for God's sake. That's what I asked for!"

Once again my confidence got me in trouble.

Paradise Island

CHAPTER NINE

Networking with Health Professionals

In the resources section at the end of this book I've listed the telephone numbers of organizations that can be helpful in a crisis, along with other organizations, such as MIND, where you can become a member and attend regular meetings. I find it useful to be a member of organizations such as this, as you meet like-minded people and can share how you are feeling in a safe environment.

To build a successful relationship with your health care team, it is a good idea to know your entitlements as a patient. The following is what you are legally entitled to as a patient in the UK:

- All correspondence with health professionals must be copied to the patient.
- The patient can ask for copies of records through the Freedom of Information Act.
- As a patient you have rights under data protection. Health professionals are not allowed to disclose to third parties (unless there is immediate risk to self or others).
- As a patient, you have the right to ask for a carer's assessment.
- There is a complaints procedure policy, and you should know how to make a complaint.
- As a patient you have the right to make an advance directive about care and declare what you don't want in your care plan.
- As a patient you are entitled to regular CPA meetings at least

once a year, with you being involved in devising a care plan.

- You should have care review meetings as required to look at general mental health well-being.
- There should be discussions with your care coordinator about self-directed support and personal budgets to meet eligible needs.
- As a patient, you should be given clear and complete information about medication and its side effects (verbally and in writing).
- As a patient you should be involved in deciding what treatment is appropriate and ask for alternative treatments to be considered.

In order to build successful relationships with health professionals you need to do the following:

- Be honest and direct about your personal journey. Best outcomes for you will come when health professionals know the facts.
- Meet the health professionals half way by listening to the advice being given.
- Adhere to the parts of the care plan that you are responsible for.
- Take responsibility for improving your own lifestyle and general health. For example, making sure you eat well, exercise, avoid illicit drugs and excessive alcohol, and ensure you have a regular sleep pattern.
- You need to be aware of your key indicators and that they are clear for both the mental health team and you, the patient.
- You need to draw up a clear crisis contingency plan, which should include who to contact and contact details.

- Be reliable in attending appointments, CPA review meetings.
- You need to fully follow guidance given by a psychiatrist about medication. Do not change medication or stop medication without seeking professional medical advice.

By following the advice of the above, it will help you in building relationships with the health professionals you come in contact with.

Best Way to Handle Doctors

You have to be prepared to challenge the mental health professionals in charge of your care and not readily accept all the drugs they offer you. It is important to listen to their advice and come to an agreement on the best way forward, once you have received all the information.

It's easy to feel intimidated by the status and knowledge of the medical profession, but the reality is that *you* have the most knowledge about your illness because you are the one who lives with it. Remember: doctors tend to listen to you more if you can show that you have insight into your illness.

Keeping Your Family and Friends in the Loop

Involve as many members of your family or friends in your CPA and review meetings as you can. It may be that you get on with one member of the family or one friend much better than others. This is fine. It's important to get the right people involved in your care plan. Think about who you see on a regular basis—it's not helpful to have a friend who lives miles from you and who only sees you on an irregular basis be involved in the CPA. They may not be able to make informed decisions, as they are not seeing you on a regular basis. Choose people who are able to offer helpful feedback on your mental health, as this will allow your health care team to work with you more effectively.

I remember my children once stopped me having a manic episode. They had started to notice that I could not stop cleaning, and they knew that obsessive cleaning is one of my key indicators. They called my sister Kay, who came over immediately. She sat down with me and got me to see that I was in a hypomanic state and unwell. During our subsequent conversation, I explained that I had stopped taking my medication. My sister got in touch with my care coordinator straight away, and my mental health team took control. This would have gone undetected if it weren't for the children raising the alarm. Family and friends are essential in helping keeping you well.

CHAPTER TEN

Transformation

I am now a mature woman and I can honestly say that bipolar is my friend and not my foe. Why do I say that? Because, during my journey with the illness, I have been transformed from a creative, whacky young woman into a woman with character and courage. Each episode of Bipolar leaves me feeling more exhausted yet enriched. After my three stays in psychiatric hospitals, each time I have returned to the community stronger and more open to ideas. What enables me to be stronger is my attitude towards the illness and the support and care I receive from health professionals, family, and friends. This isn't to negate the seriousness of the illness and how sometimes it is the enemy.

I have had five episodes of mania that have required the crisis care team visit my home. Each episode has been a reminder that bipolar is a lifelong illness that I have to come to terms with. With the help of my crisis care team, I have come to understand that I need to not treat bipolar as the enemy, that I will get well again, and that these attacks are not permanent. To live with bipolar disorder, you have to see the condition as your friend, so you are not frightened by it. What we fear we give our power to and can become immobilized by it.

When I interviewed people with bipolar for this book, many of them were terrified by their illness—so much so, they hardly ever went out into the community. They lacked the confidence to try to work. In fact, a large number of people with mental illness do not work due to this reason.

After losing my business in 2009, I didn't have a regular job for two years, although I did do some work for Kent County Council and Lambeth Council and I painted and wrote. Not having regular work negatively impacted my mental health to a certain extent: we need structure to our day, and work provides that. Whilst keeping my hand in and doing occasional work was very important, it is only now that I have regular part-time work that I have found my mental health has improved immensely.

Working with your mind so that you see bipolar as your friend can really help you learn to live with the condition. It is, after all, mind over matter. The more you can embrace the situation, the more confident you become. This is when I use affirmations to help me remain positive.

There have been times when I have not had such a rosy view of things. When I go into a psychiatric hospital, I am away from my family and friends for over six weeks at a time. This is a long stretch for young children. I always remember my son, who was only four in 2004, asking my sister Kay how many lunches and dinners he would need to eat before Mummy was home. My daughter Brooke, who was seven at the time, spent every day writing me letters whilst I was in hospital. Megan, my eldest daughter, brought her friends to see me to help me focus on coming home.

There is no doubt that the illness can tear families apart. They do not see bipolar disorder as a friend; they see it as the enemy. My experience has been that it is harder for people around me to cope than it is for me, the person with the illness.

I think people who suffer the lows more than the highs will find it difficult to see bipolar as a friend. I know that when I am severely depressed, I hate the illness and see it as my enemy. Depression is such a wicked illness, leaving the person and everyone around them feeling helpless. At these times, I am not so optimistic about the illness.

What I have learnt from experience is that after a journey with the "black cloud" in tow, I feel so much better about life when it lifts. I recognize I am coming out of a depression by the way I look at life and the colours I am able to see. When I'm depressed, everything is black, but once the cloud has lifted, I am able to see colours in all their glory.

The sky isn't just blue; it is vivid. The sun isn't just yellow; it is a ball of fire. Colours are majestically heightened.

For the majority of us, this illness is not life threatening. Some people cannot cope with the highs and lows of the illness and do, unfortunately, take their own lives. The majority, though, recover from each episode and are able to lead a normal life.

One skilful way of managing this illness is to keep a record of your highs and lows, so you can be prepared where possible. Being around optimistic people is a must. Believe in yourself, know that you will survive the storm, and trust that the periods of mental health will far outnumber episodes of being unwell.

Case Studies of Patients Who Live Successfully with Bipolar

I wanted an opportunity to talk to a selection of people who see the illness as enabling and give them great momentum in their life.

Jackie, who is 21 years old, said the following:

> I always knew I was different, very different. I come from a large family of five children. My three sisters and my brother all seemed really boring compared to me. They never seemed to question anything. They never seemed to go anywhere.
>
> I belonged to our local church because I enjoyed drama and they put on a good show every season. I played everything, from Mary to musicals. It was great fun. Often, when I played these parts, I would be high, but no one would really notice because I was a child and I was expected to be enjoying myself. I was really good at acting.
>
> My problems started when I went to secondary school and I found it hard to concentrate in lessons. I remember one day my

teacher asked me to come and write something on the board — an answer to a maths question — and I wrote "P*** off" instead. This is when they first noticed something was not quite right. I was 15 years old. I have to say my classmates' reaction was one of horror, but I was the centre of attention!!

It didn't bother me because I felt fantastic most of the time, and my outbursts just helped a boring lesson get more interesting.

At 15, I did lose the plot, and sat in the toilets at school punching my body to pulp. This episode took me to hospital and I was diagnosed with bipolar disorder. I have to say, when the doctors told me about the illness I was quite scared, first of all. I now know I have nothing to be frightened of.

I think I have a lot to be thankful for because I am very creative. I play the piano to a very high level, and it is my goal to become a pianist. I love to write music and hope to be recognized one day. I have a good circle of friends and strong family life. I find my illness very enabling.

Meeting Christine was a real joy:

I was diagnosed with bipolar when I was 27. I am now 45, and I can honestly say I have embraced my illness and I can value the many benefits that bipolar can bring.

I got married when I was 29 and didn't tell my husband that I was bipolar. I was worried he wouldn't be able to cope and he would run in the opposite direction. I always remember when I had my first manic attack, my husband was at work and I had been running fast for a month or so.

My husband didn't recognize the signs because he had always known me to be like this. I was in the garden and I started talking to the plants, talking to God, and singing at the top of my voice.

A neighbour came to the rescue, and I was sectioned for four weeks. I tell you this because I am embarrassed that I ever lied to my husband. He now fully understands the illness and is 100 percent supportive.

I am lucky because I only really suffer from the highs. I don't know what I would do with a depression around. I am very creative; I enjoy arts and crafts and playing the cello. I don't like having bipolar. I love it!

Graham tells his story:

I am a large personality with a big heart, according to my wife and children. I am a musician and play abroad in Europe on a regular basis. I have always been creative and felt that I have always been bipolar. I was diagnosed with the illness six years ago. I am now 36.

I have chosen to go down the alternative route and not take lithium or antipsychotic drugs. I look after myself by a healthy diet with lots of fish and pulses. I often go into mania, but I have a loving wife who looks after me.

I don't believe I would be able to produce music to the level I do without bipolar. My children are often frightened by my mood swings, which are very upsetting. I do my best to reassure them. I have been in a psychiatric ward once in my life, and would not like to return.

Harry is an interesting man:

I'm now 65 years old and am still very active in the community. I run a Boy's Brigade club for the local children in London. I have been in hospital six times in my life span. Each episode was for a manic attack.

I've been highly creative all my life and spent most of my time as a professional artist. I am single and never had children, so I have been allowed to be rather selfish with the illness.

I have always believed in fate and never to argue the hand you have been dealt. I strongly believe in God and everything is for a reason. It's not for us to question and the illness is not too bad anyway.

If the truth were known I am very happy with my lot. There is nothing to fear when you receive a diagnosis of bipolar.

Adrian tells his story:

I've suffered with more lows than highs, and it does drive me mad, but after every low I feel more confident to achieve the next task in my life.

I am married with three young children. I am 30 and was diagnosed ten years ago, after my one and only manic occurrence that led me into hospital.

I run my own computer company, and all the team know I am bipolar. This is good because when I suffer a depression the team are behind me to help me through it. They also cover my work, whilst I am off recovering from the depression. I think it's essential to tell work colleagues, especially the boss, so they can be supportive through each episode.

I know my illness causes more of a strain for my friends and family, as they constantly have to watch me unwell. As I've said, for me I can see the positives in the illness. I know I will come out the other side stronger and more creative because of the black cloud.

I wouldn't give bipolar away, though I would ask for less down time. Experiencing the highs more would be great.

Finding the Strength to Continue to
Grow After Each Manic Episode

It definitely seems that the experience of bipolar highs as opposed to lows is beneficial, even though we have heard how productive you can be after a low. One thing is common, no matter where you fall on the pole: After each episode of bipolar, you are left exhausted and vulnerable and need time to readjust and pick up the pieces.

After my first manic episode, in 2004, it took me nine months to recover fully. My recovery was aided by doing the things I have described in this book—improving my diet, correcting my medication, doing regular exercise, participating in hobbies, and seeing family and friends.

It's interesting that it took me nine months to recover and it takes nine months to give birth to a new life. In a way, I felt my recovery time allowed me to heal from the traumas I experienced and be reborn. During recovery, it is important that you believe that you will get well again. You have the power to make anything happen.

Part of mania is the build-up from hypomania to mania. It can take several weeks for mania to reach its pinnacle, and then you run so fast you either burn out or have to be heavily sedated. It is because of this that recovery takes so long. It is a slow process.

Someone who has had a manic episode has often experienced really weird things and could have offended lots of people on the journey. Mania can be frightening because it often comes with psychosis, and that can be when you lose mental capacity. This does not always happen. Each person's journey with bipolar disorder is unique. Know that you will get better again.

Bipolar disorder is only part of you and not the whole. It can be highly creative and a wonderful place to be. You must learn to embrace bipolar and not fear it. Trust that you will survive the highs and the lows and through each episode you will become stronger.

— *LYNN HODGES*

Recommended Reading

Albrecht, Ava T. and Charles Herrick. *100 Questions and Answers About Bipolar Disorder*. Burlington, MA: Jones and Bartlett Publishers, 2007.

Fast, Julie A. and John Preston. *Take Charge of Bipolar Disorder*. New York, NY: Warner Wellness, 2006.

Fink, Candida and Joe. *Bipolar Disorder For Dummies*. New York, NY: John Wiley Publishing, 2005.

Jamison, Kay Redfield. *An Unquiet Mind*. New York, NY: Alfred A Knopf, 1995.

_____. *Night Falls Fast*. New York, NY: Vintage Books, 2000.

_____. *Touched With Fire: Manic Depressive Illness and the Artistic Temperament*. New York, NY: The Free Press (a division of MacMillan), 1993.

Marohn, Stephanie. *The Natural Medicine Guide to Bipolar Disorder*. Charlottesville, VA: Hampton Roads Publishing, 2003.

Mondimore, F. M. *Bipolar Disorder: A Guide for Patients and Families*. Johns Hopkins University Press, 2006.

Miklowitz, David J. *The Bipolar Disorder Survival Guide*. Baltimore, MD: The Guilford Press, 2010.

Owen, Sarah and Amanda Saunders. *Bipolar Disorder – The Ultimate Guide*. One World Publications, 2008.

Papolos, D. F and J. Papolos. *The Bipolar Child*. New York, NY: Broadway Books, 2006.

Sutherland, S. *Breakdown*. Oxford, UK: Oxford University Press, 1998.

Weil, Andrew M.D., *Spontaneous Happiness*. Boston, MA: Little Brown and Company 2011.

Useful Websites

www.myhealingkitchen.com. A well-researched website aimed at healing medical conditions with whole foods, including Depression. Studies backing up nutritional claims are linked for each article, and there are lots of great recipes and ideas to support health, too.

www.whfoods.org. This nonprofit organization is focused on educating the public about the health qualities of different foods. Each entry has very complete information.

Organizations Working
With Mental Health

England

Advance Housing and Support Ltd

2 Witan Way, Witney OX28 6FH

Tel: 01993 772 885

info@advanceuk.org

www.advanceuk.org

Places to live for people with mental health problems.

Anxiety UK

Zion Community Resource Centre

339 Stretford Road, Hulme, Manchester M15 4ZY

Tel: 08444 775 774

info@anxietyuk.org.uk

www.anxietyuk.org.uk

Support services and self-help groups for sufferers of all anxiety disorders.

Arbours Association

Arbours Psychotherapy service,

6 Church Lane, London NB 7BU

Tel: 0208 340 7646

info@arboursassociation.org

www.arboursassociation.org

Offers psychotherapeutic support for individuals.

Association for Post-Natal Illness
145 Dawes Road,
London SW6 7EB
Tel: 0207 386 0868
www.apni.org
Provides support for individuals who suffer post-natal depression.

Beat
(Eating Disorders Association)
103 Prince of Wales Road,
Norwich, Norfolk NR1 1DW
Tel: 01603 619 090
help@b-eat.co.uk
www.b-eat.co.uk
Help and support for people affected by eating disorders.

Bipolar UK
(formerly MDF The Bipolar Organisation England)
11 Belgrave Road,
London SW1V 1RB
Tel: 0207 931 6480
www.bipolaruk.org.uk, info@bipolaruk.org.uk
National charity dedicated to supporting people with bipolar disorder.

Centre for Better Health
1A Darnley Road,
London E9 6QH
Tel: 0208 985 3570
www.centreforbetterhealth.org.uk
Services, training, and research.

Centre for Mental Health
134-138 Borough High Street,
London SE1 1LB
Tel: 0207 827 8300
www.centreformentalhealth.org.uk
Information from an organization aiming to improve the quality of life for people with severe mental health problems.

Combat Stress
Tywhitt House, Oaklawn Road,
Leatherhead KT22 OBX
Tell: 01372 841600
contactus@combatstress.org.uk
www.combatstress.org.uk
Local area support details via website.

Depression Alliance
20 Great Dover Street, London SE1 4LX
Tel: 0845 123 2320
information@depressionalliance.org
www.depressionalliance.org
Provides information and support for depression.

Depression UK
c/o Self Help Nottingham, Ormiston House,
32-36 Pelham Street,
Nottingham NG1 2EG
info@depressionuk.org
www.depressionuk.org
Promoting mutual support for those affected by or at risk from depression.

Hearing Voices Network

c/o Sheffield Hearing Voices Network,
Limbrick Day Service, Limbrick Road, Sheffield S6 2PE
Tel: 0114 271 8210
info@hearing-voices.org
www.hearing-voices.org
Hearing Voices offers 180 support groups in communities throughout England.

Mental Health Foundation England

9th Floor, Sea Containers House,
20 Upper Ground, London SE1 9QB
Tel: 0207 803 1101
mhf@mhf.org.uk
www.mentalhealth.org.uk
A charity improving the lives of those with mental health problems or learning disabilities.

Mental Health Tribunal Service

Headquarters
PO Box 8793, 5th Floor, Leicester LE1 6LR
Tel: 0116 249 4357
www.mhrt.org.uk
Offers support with mental health issues.

MIND (National Association for Mental Health)

Head Office, 15-19 Broadway, London E15 4BQ
Tel: 0208 519 2122
contact@mind.org.uk
www.mind.org.uk
The leading mental health charity for England and Wales.

NICE

MidCity Place
71 High Holborn
London WC1V 6NA
Tel: 0845 0037 780
nice@nice.org.uk
www.nice.org.uk
Providing quality standards and other guidance for social care in England.

Rethink – Head Office

89 Albert Embankment, London SE1 7TP
Tel: 0845 456 0455
ifo@rethink.org
www.rethink.org
National mental health charity, information, services, and a strong voice for everyone affected by mental illness.

Richmond Fellowship

80 Holloway Road, London N7 8JG
Tel: 0207 697 3300
communications@richmondfellowship.org.uk
www.richmondfellowship.org.uk
Housing, care, and support.

Royal College of Psychiatrists

17 Belgrave Square, London SW1X 8PG
Tel: 0207 235 2351
rcpsych@rcpsych.ac.uk
www.rcpsych.ac.uk
The online mental health resource for the public and professionals.

Rural Stress Helpline

Arthur Rank Centre, Stoneleigh Park,
Warwickshire CV8 2LG
Tel: 0845 094 8286
help@ruralstresshelpline.co.uk
www.ruralstresshelpline.co.uk
Helping rural people experiencing stress/mental health and well-being
problems.

Sane

1st Floor, Cityside House, 40 Adler Street,
London E1 1EE
Tel: 0207 375 1002
info@sane.org.uk
www.sane.org.uk
Meeting the challenge of mental illness.

Seasonal Affective Disorder Association (SAD)

PO Box 989, Steyning BN44 3HG
www.sada.org.uk
A small UK voluntary organization dedicated to helping people combat the symptoms of seasonal affective disorder.

Together: Working for Wellbeing

National Office, 12 Old Street,
London EC1V 9BE
Tel: 0207 780 7300
contactus@together-uk.org
www.together-uk.org
A national mental health charity working alongside people with mental health issues.

Young Minds
Suite 11,
Baden Place,
Crosby Row,
London SE1 1YW
Tel: 0207 089 5050
www.youngminds.org.uk
Improving the mental health of all children.

**Secure Forensic Mental Health
Service for Young People**
Birmingham & Solihull Mental Health Trust
Ardenleigh Medium Secure Unit,
385 Kingsbury Road, Erdington,
Birmingham B24 9SA
Tel: 0121 678 4400
A 20-bed facility for young male and female patients.

Bolton, Salford & Trafford Mental Health Trust
The Gardener Unit, Bury New Road,
Prestwich, Manchester M25 3BL
Tel: 0161 772 3425/6
A 10-bed facility for young male patients only.

Hampshire Partnership NHS Trust
Bluebird House Adolescent Unit, Maple
Buildings, Calmore, Tatchbury Mount
Hospital, Southampton SO40 2RZ
Tel: 023 8087 4600
Cares for both young male and female patients.

Newcastle, North Tyneside & Northumberland Mental Health Trust

Roycroft Unit, 1st Floor, St Nicholas House,
St Nicholas Hospital, Jubilee Road,
Newcastle NE3 3XT
Tel: 0191 223 2226
An18-bed facility for young male and female patients.

South London & Maudsley Trust

Bill Yule Adolescent Unit, Tyson West 1,
Bethlehem Royal Hospital, Monks Orchard Road,
Beckenham BR3 3BX
Tel: 0203 228 4652
A 10-bed facility for young male and female patients.

West London Mental Health Trust

The Wells Unit, Three Bridges Secure Unit,
Uxbridge Road, Southall UB1 3EU
Tel: 0208 483 2270/020 Ward
A 10-bed facility for young male patients.

Scotland

Action on Depression

11 Alva Street, Edinburgh EH2 4PH
Tel: 0808 802 2020
info@dascot.org
www.dascot.org
The only national charity working specifically with and for people affected by depression in Scotland.

Mental Health Foundation

Merchants House,
30 George Square,
Glasgow G2 1EG
Tel: 0141 572 0125
Scotland@mhf.org.uk
A mental health foundation concerned with both mental health issues and learning disabilities.

MHTS Scotland Headquarters

First Floor, Bothwell House,
Hamilton Business Park,
Caird Park,
Hamilton ML3 0QA
Tel: 0800 345 7060
mhts@scotland.gsi.gov.uk
www.mhtscotland.gov.uk
Provides a responsive and accessible, independent and impartial service to help make decisions on the compulsory care and treatment of people with mental disorders.

Mental Welfare Commission for Scotland

Thistle House,
91 Haymarket Terrace,
Edinburgh EH12 5HE
Tel: 0800 389 6809
enquiries@mwcscot.org.uk
www.mwcscot.org.uk
An independent organisation working to safeguard the rights and welfare of everyone with a mental illness, learning disability or other mental disorder.

Support In Mind Scotland
(formerly National Schizophrenia Fellowship (Scotland)
6 Newington Business Centre, Dalkeith
Road Mews, Edinburgh EH16 5GA
Tel: 0131 662 4359
n.cortada@supportinmindscotland.org.uk
www.supportinmindscotland.org.uk
Offers profile of group mental health laws, forms, resources and contracts, information and able to signpost other organizations and caring
agencies.

SAMH Information Service
Brunswick House,
51 Wilson Street,
Glasgow G1 1UZ
Tel: 0141 530 1000
enquire@samh.org.uk
www.samh.org.uk
Scotland's leading mental health charity.

Wales

**Journeys (Formally Depression Alliance
Cymru)**
120-122 Broadway, Roath,
Cardiff CF24 2NJ
Tel: 029 2069 2891
info@journeysonline.org.uk
www.journeysonline.org.uk
Supporting people finding their route from depression.

MDF The Bipolar Organisation Cymru
Floor 4, Clarence House, Clarence Place,
Newport,
Gwent NP19 7AA
Tel: 01633 244 244
info@mdfwales.org.uk
www.mdfwales.org.uk
A user-led organization for people with bipolar disorder (manic depression).

MHF Wales
Merlin House, No 1 Langstone Business Park,
Priory Drive, Newport NP18 2HJ
Tel: 01633 415 434
walesMHF@mhf.org.uk
Charity improving the lives of those with mental health problems or learning disabilities.

Wales Office
Mental Health Tribunal Service for Wales
Crown Buildings, Cathays Park, Cardiff CF10 3NQ
Tel: 0845 223 2022
www.mhrt.org.uk
Tribunal service.

Mind Cymru
3rd Floor, Quebec House, 5-19 Cowbridge
Road East, Cardiff CF11 9AB
Tel: 029 2039 5123
www.mind.org.uk
The leading mental health charity for England and Wales.

Northern Ireland

Northern Ireland Association for Mental Health
Central Office, 80 University Street, Belfast BT7 1HE
Tel: 028 9032 8474
info@niamhwellbeing.org
www.niamh.co.uk
Mental health and well-being for all.

United States

The Balanced Mind Foundation
www.bpkids.org
The Balanced Mind Foundation improves the lives of families raising children and teens living with bipolar disorder and related conditions.

Depression & Bipolar Support Alliance
www.dbsalliance.org
Offers information on depression and bipolar disorder as well as listings to patient support groups across the USA.

International Society for Bipolar Disorders
www.isbd.org
Improving the lives of those with bipolar disorder through collaboration, research, and education.

National Alliance on Mental Illness
www.nami.org
NAMI is the largest organization for people with mental illness in the United States.

Canada

Mood Disorders Association of British Columbia
www.MDABC.net
An organization that provides support to family and friends.

Mood Disorders Association of Ontario
www.mooddisorders.ca
The Association helps people with Bipolar and their family and friends.

Mood Disorders Society of Canada
www.mooddisorderscanada.ca
MDSC is a web-based organization set up to help people with depression and Bipolar Disorder.

Australia

SANE Australia
www.sane.org
A national charitable organization for the mentally ill.

New Zealand

Balance NZ Bipolar & Depression Network
www.balance.org.nz
This organization provides support services for people with depression and Bipolar Disorder.

Bipolar Support @ MHAPS
www.bipolarsupportcanterbury.org.nz
This organization is for people with Bipolar Disorder and their families.

About the Author

Lynn Hodges is the founder of Up Front, a company that specialized in teaching people presentation, public speaking, leadership, and management coaching skills.

Lynn was diagnosed with bipolar disorder in 2004. She has a unique understanding of her condition, which enables her to offer her expertise to others. She now runs Creative Coaching Consultancy, which specializes in working with doctors, psychiatrists, social workers, and all those involved with mental health to help them understand what it is like to live with bipolar disorder.

Her intention in writing this book is to reach out to many bipolar sufferers and their families around the world and to give them hope that there is life after being diagnosed with bipolar disorder.

She is also a single mother of three beautiful children, of whom she is very proud.

More information on Lynn can be found on her websites *www. livingwithbipolardisorder.co.uk* and *lynnhodgesart.co.uk.*

About the Paintings

I started painting in 2004, the same year I had my first manic attack. Over the years I have found art to be a great comfort to me and a way to express my feelings. I was introduced to painting in oils by a professional artist, Alexis, who showed me the importance of colour.

In the book you will see several prints that express different moods depicting where I was on the bipolar pole when I created them: *The Evacuee* (p. 10), *Masked* (p. 28), *Talking Heads* (p. 36), *A Walk in the Woods* (p. 93), *Fly High* (p. 104), and *Paradise Island* (p. 114).

When I am manic I paint furiously with a feeling of urgency inside. These paintings express all the emotions I am feeling, from passion to sadness. On the flip side, when I am depressed I paint in much more detail and tend to move towards figures to express my emotions.

I spend most of my time painting alone and each picture will be unique as it will be from my imagination and not taken from another artist or impression. I have also painted with fellow artists and enjoy the companionship this offers.

The great thing about my art is that it helps me communicate to family and friends, and the health professional, how I am feeling at a particular time.

I hope you enjoy the selection of prints we have used for this book, if you are interested in seeing more of my work please visit my website, *lynnhodgesart.co.uk.*

— *Lynn*

FINDHORN PRESS

Life-Changing Books

For a complete catalogue,
please contact:

Findhorn Press Ltd
117-121 High Street,
Forres IV36 1AB,
Scotland, UK

t +44 (0)1309 690582
f +44 (0)131 777 2711
e info@findhornpress.com

or consult our catalogue online
(with secure order facility) on
www.findhornpress.com

For information on the Findhorn Foundation:
www.findhorn.org